ADELPHI
Paper • 299

A US Strategy for the Asia-Pacific

Contents

Oxford University Press, Walton Street, Oxford OX2 6DP
Oxford New York
Athens Auckland Bangkok Bombay
Calcutta Cape Town Dar es Salaam Delhi
Florence Hong Kong Istanbul Karachi
Kuala Lumpur Madras Madrid Melbourne
Mexico City Nairobi Paris Singapore
Taipei Tokyo Toronto
and associated companies in
Berlin Ibadan

Oxford is a trade mark of Oxford University Press

Published in the United States
by Oxford University Press Inc., New York

© The International Institute for Strategic Studies 1995

First published December 1995 by Oxford University Press for
The International Institute for Strategic Studies
23 Tavistock Street, London WC2E 7NQ

Director: Dr John Chipman
Deputy Director: Rose Gottemoeller
Assistant Editor: Juliet Sampson

British Library Cataloguing in Publication Data

Data available

Library of Congress Cataloging in Publication Data

ISBN 0-19-829073-X
ISSN 0567-932X

GLOSSARY

ANZUS	Australia–New Zealand–US
APEC	Asia-Pacific Economic Cooperation
ARF	ASEAN Regional Forum
ASEAN	Association of South-East Asian Nations
AWACS	airborne warning and control system
C³I	command, control, communications and intelligence
DMZ	demilitarised zone
DPG	Defense Planning Guidance Statement (US)
DPRK	Democratic People's Republic of Korea (North Korea)
EAEC	East Asian Economic Caucus
EASI	East Asia Strategic Initiative
EEP	Export Enhancement Program
EEZ	Exclusive Economic Zone
FPDA	Five Power Defence Arrangement
G-7	Group of Seven
GATT	General Agreement on Tariffs and Trade
GDP	gross domestic product
GPALS	global protection against limited strikes
IMF	International Monetary Fund
JSTARS	joint strategic airborne reconnaissance system
MST	Mutual Security Treaty
NAFTA	North American Free Trade Agreement
NGO	non-governmental organisation
PACOM	Pacific Command (US)
PECC	Pacific Economic Cooperation Council
PLA	People's Liberation Army
PLAN	People's Liberation Army Navy
PRC	People's Republic of China
RIMPAC	Rim of the Pacific
ROK	Republic of Korea (South Korea)
SDF	Self-Defense Force (Japan)
TRA	Taiwan Relations Act
UNCLOS	United Nations Convention on the Law of the Sea
USFK	United States Forces, Korea
WTO	World Trade Organisation

INTRODUCTION

> Peace requires either hegemony or balance of power. We have neither the resources nor the stomach for the former. The only question is how much we have to suffer before we realize it.
>
> Henry Kissinger, 1988

Sometime in the not-too-distant future the United States will no longer be in a position to guarantee the stability of the Asia-Pacific by its unilateral actions and forward military presence. In the next ten years, the US-dominated system of Asia-Pacific security that evolved during the Cold War must be fundamentally transformed. Public commitments by both the Bush and Clinton administrations to maintain US military forces in Asia, and the strong support that many Asian states have shown for a continued US presence, are short-term indicators inconsistent with the trends that will ultimately determine the region's security in the future.

One of these trends is the growing economic and military power of key Asian states which will increasingly allow them to resist US influence. Another trend is the US public's grudging acceptance of the limitations of US power in a post-Cold War world. With luck, this national consensus can be channelled into support for a new and more collaborative approach to US foreign policy. But it is at least as likely that the national mood will evolve into a prickly and resentful form of isolationism.

There are a number of steps the United States can take in the next decade to contribute to a multipolar balance-of-power system in which the interactions of Asian states are conditioned by a general interest in war avoidance and a region-wide acceptance of the need for economic and political cooperation. Achieving this goal will be difficult, but not impossible.

A multipolar regional order will be less open to US interests and influence than is the web of bilateral defence arrangements that has persisted for the last four decades. The 'San Francisco system' was initiated in September 1951 when the United States entered into a number of treaties (all signed in San Francisco) with Asia-Pacific states: the Mutual Security Treaty (MST) with Japan; the Mutual Defence Treaty with the Philippines; and the Australia–New Zealand–US (ANZUS) accord. The alliance network was subsequently expanded to include South Korea (in 1953), Taiwan (in 1954, abrogated in the wake of the normalisation of US–China relations), and Thailand (in 1962, with the Rusk–Thanat communiqué). The San Francisco system, however, simply cannot survive into the twenty-first century and must be supplanted by some form of multipolar balancing of power. In these circumstances, the best policy for the United States is to undertake initiatives designed to make this new arrangement as benign and reliable as possible.

During the next decade, the United States would be well advised to exploit its residual influence in Asia to help sponsor new institutions and patterns of behaviour that will facilitate regional cooperation and conflict resolution. To achieve this, American policy-makers need a clear sense of post-Cold War US interests in the Asia-Pacific and an appreciation of where these interests converge with and diverge from the interests of key regional actors. The United States will also have to accord a much higher priority to the nation most likely to present a revisionist challenge in the Asia-Pacific region – China. Confronting and establishing a new *modus vivendi* with the People's Republic of China (PRC) will be extraordinarily difficult, but there is no practical or responsible alternative for US foreign policy in the twenty-first century.

I. POST-COLD WAR US DEFENCE POLICY IN ASIA

Lord Salisbury once observed that the most common political error is 'sticking to the carcasses of dead policies'. This tendency is identifiable among those policy-makers responsible for planning the United States' post-Cold War defence posture in the Asia-Pacific. The posture statements of both the Bush and Clinton administrations reflect the logic of 'more of the same, for less'. These statements are unanimous on three mutually inconsistent points: that the Asia-Pacific region is undergoing dramatic structural change; that the US has had to reduce the size of its Asia-based forces to meet established budget targets; and that the San Francisco system of US-dominated bilateral treaties must be preserved as the primary source of Asia-Pacific security.

The original rationale for the San Francisco system is no longer appropriate in a world where the Soviet Union has disappeared, Asia has become a nexus of global trade and investment, and local political disputes have supplanted ideological struggles as the main threats to security. In such an environment, the United States has two vital interests in Asia: preventing one or more regional powers from posing a direct military threat to the United States or its key allies; and building US economic prosperity by improving US access to the dynamic economies of the region.

The United States will have difficulty advancing and protecting these vital interests if it continues to cling to the San Francisco system as the basis for its regional security posture. Efforts by the Bush and Clinton administrations to preserve the Cold War framework in Asia illustrate the problem.

Defence Planning Under Bush and Clinton

Both the Bush and Clinton administrations have grappled with the problem of redefining US security interests in the Asia-Pacific. The Bush administration's strategic planning process was essentially budget-driven, while the Clinton administration's approach has been influenced primarily by the 1991 Gulf War, and conditioned by budgetary and domestic political considerations. The theme that runs throughout the efforts of both administrations to fashion a post-Cold War US strategy for the Asia-Pacific is the priority accorded to the delivery of a 'peace dividend' to US citizens. Accordingly, both administrations struggled to reconcile cuts in defence spending with an Asian security posture that still lay within the San Francisco framework.

The Bush Administration

The Bush administration's ability to engage in a comprehensive reassessment of US interests was hindered by the transitional nature of world politics, particularly the dangers associated with the Soviet Union's death throes. Whatever the reasons, caution and policy continuity were the hallmarks of the Bush administration's initial approach to post-Cold War foreign-policy planning. The theme of continuity was developed for the Asia-Pacific by then Secretary of State James Baker, who in 1991 argued that the US-sponsored system of bilateral alliances was still indispensable as a basis for regional order, comparing the network of alliances to 'a fan spread wide, with its base in North America'.[1]

A disruption to Sino-American relations following the Chinese government's 1989 crackdown in Tiananmen Square made it difficult for Baker to speculate on change in the Asia-Pacific region. It was a reflection of US ambivalence that Baker ranked China fifth in a list of US 'critical relationships' in Asia – after Japan, Korea, South-east Asia and Australia. Without a coherent vision for Sino-American relations, other elements of the administration's policy towards Asia were unclear. This lack of clear strategic vision tended to reinforce the administration's instinct to maintain the *status quo*.

In May 1992, the Bush administration completed its new Regional Defense Strategy as part of its 1994–99 *Defense Planning Guidance* (DPG).[2] The Strategy focused on one overriding goal: preventing any hostile power from dominating the European and Asia-Pacific regions. The DPG differed in important respects from plans put forward in an earlier draft. The draft, which was leaked to the *New York Times*, called for a 'strategy of preponderance' to block any challenges to US global pre-eminence.[3] By the end of 1992, in the face of concerted Congressional opposition and criticism from US friends and allies, the DPG was modified to place greater emphasis on working with regional allies to preserve post-Cold War order.[4] This doctrinal revision was welcomed in Asia, in particular because any attempt by the United States to achieve unipolar dominance in the region would have unnecessarily exacerbated tensions with China and laid the groundwork for a new bilateral confrontation in the Asia-Pacific.

To implement the Regional Defense Strategy the Bush administration applied its Base Force plan, developed throughout 1990, for downsizing and reconfiguring overall military strength.[5] Downsizing was, in fact, the key element of the plan, which was at core an attempt to respond to growing domestic political pressures for defence cuts. The administration argued that reductions in the defence budget could be compensated for by a military posture that effectively combined four elements: reconstitution; forward presence; crisis response; and strategic deterrence and defence. In a regional context this meant that, above all, alliance commitments in Europe and Asia would be preserved and ballistic-missile defences would be developed to shield US forward-deployed and allied forces from limited missile attacks.[6]

The Base Force plan was applied to the Asia-Pacific region in the East Asia Strategic Initiative (EASI). EASI, a Bush administration posture statement, was first introduced in April 1990 and was updated in July 1992 in the EASI-II report.[7] In accordance with the logic of the Regional Defense Strategy, EASI assumed that a global war with Asian battle lines was no longer likely. Limited contingencies in which US forces could be introduced to confront threats to US access and influence in the region were, however, anticipated. The Pacific Force was to be geared towards tactical naval and air missions related to the defence of Japan and South Korea. More generally, challenges to US regional access and influence were to be prevented or deterred.

The Base Force/EASI-directed Pacific Force assumed phased reductions in US force strength in the Asia-Pacific of 10–12% initially, or around 15,000 personnel out of the approximately 135,000 stationed in the region in 1990. Over a ten-year period, further force-strength reductions were to be implemented, reducing US forces in the region to just over 100,000 (Table 1).[8]

The only real setback to the timetable outlined by the first EASI was a freeze in withdrawing an additional 6,000 troops from South Korea in November 1991 after an initial pull-out of nearly 7,000. Intelligence reports concerning North Korea's possible development of nuclear-weapons capabilities convinced US defence planners that a larger US deterrent tripwire was temporarily required on the Korean peninsula.

A 'more widely distributed' US force presence in South-east Asia was also anticipated, to compensate for the loss of access to Clark Air Base and Subic Naval Base in the Philippines (Table 2). Various defence-related agreements were signed or upgraded with Singapore (where the US Seventh Fleet's Logistics Support Force was moved from the Philippines), Malaysia, Brunei and Thailand. In accordance with its theme of policy continuity, the Bush administration treated the departure from the Philippines as a routine adjustment to the changing strategic environment in the Asia-Pacific, although US

8

Table 1:   Phased US Troop Reductions in the Asia-Pacific

COUNTRY Service	1990 Starting Strength	Phase I Reductions 1990–1992	Philippines Withdrawal	1993 Strength	Phase II Reductions 1992–1995	1995 Strength (Approx.)
JAPAN	50,000	4,773	–	45,227	700	44,527
Army Personnel	2,000	22	–	1,978	–	1,978
Navy Shore-based	7,000	502	–	6,498	–	–
Marines	25,000	3,489	–	21,511	–	21,511
Air Force	16,000	560	–	15,440	700	14,740
Joint billets	–	200	–	–	–	–
KOREA	44,400	6,987	–	37,413	6,500[a]	30,913[a]
Army Personnel	32,000	5,000	–	27,000	–	27,000
Navy Shore-based	400	–	–	400	–	400
Marines	500	–	–	500	–	500
Air Force	11,500	1,987	–	9,513	–	9,513
PHILIPPINES	14,800	3,490	11,310	relocated elsewhere in region	–	–
Army Personnel	200	–	200		–	–
Navy Shore-based	5,000	672	4,328		–	–
Marines	900	–	900		–	–
Air Force	8,700	2,818	5,882	1,000[b]	–	1,000[b]
SUB-TOTAL	109,200	15,250	11,310	83,640	7,200	76,440
'afloat or otherwise forward deployed'	25,800			25,800		25,800
TOTAL	135,000			109,440		102,240

Source: US Department of Defense, *A Strategic Framework for the Asian Pacific Rim* (Washington DC: USGPO, 1992).

Note: The IISS is aware that the figures in this table do not tally, but they are the official figures provided by the Department of Defense.
[a] Korean troop reductions deferred in light of North Korean threat.
[b] Estimated relocations to Japan, Korea and Singapore. Does not include Guam

9

defence planners had warned for years of the direct consequences of a pull-out from the Clark and Subic facilities.

The US Defense Department characterised these force levels as 'sufficient to demonstrate that the United States will continue to be a prominent military power in the region'.[9] Its position was that by

Table 2: Bush Administration's Military Reorganisation Concept: The Pacific Force

Branch of Service	Number of Forward Deployed Elements	Number of Reserve Elements
Army	1 division (South Korea)	1 light infantry division (Hawaii or Alaska)
Navy	1 carrier battlegroup (Japan)	5 carrier battlegroups
Air Force	1–2 tactical wings (South Korea and/or Japan)	1 tactical wing (Hawaii or Alaska)
Marine Corps	1 Marine Expeditionary Force (Japan)	1–2 amphibious brigades (West Pacific and Continental United States)

Sources: The Directorate for Force Structure, Resources, and Assessment (J-8), The Joint Staff, *1992 Joint Military Net Assessment* (Washington DC: USPGO, 1992), pp. 3–7; and Research Institute for Peace and Security, Tokyo, *Asian Security 1991–92* (London: Brassey's for RIPS, 1991), p. 50.

continuing to deploy around 6% of total forces in the Asia-Pacific, the United States could still be a credible 'regional balancer' upon which Asia-Pacific states could rely for assistance with resolving or managing future crises. The key to implementing this strategy was to ensure the rapid deployment of well-equipped, mobile and flexible US units for crisis response, supported by reserve forces capable of increasing the strength of combat units during more protracted confrontations.

EASI postulated that by maintaining a substantial residual force presence within the Asia-Pacific theatre while enhancing America's ability to project power in future regional crises, the US could shape the Asia-Pacific security environment 'in ways favourable to the United States and to our allies and friends'.[10] The document also assumed that East Asia's 'economic dynamism' could be sustained; that US control of critical Asia-Pacific sea-lanes of communication could be ensured; and that the US promotion of liberal democratic values would continue throughout the region. Of particular relevance is EASI's underlying premise – that the US-dominated San Francisco system of bilateral treaties, could still be relied on to preserve US security interests in the Asia-Pacific.

The Bush administration was criticised for presenting the Base Force as a coherent response to changing conditions when, in fact, it was primarily an effort to justify defence cuts in the aftermath of the Cold War. Independent US defence analysts questioned the plan's logistical credibility, arguing that the future troop and equipment levels envisioned were too low to win another Gulf-type war or to respond quickly to lower-level crises of short duration.[11] Budget analysts, meanwhile, questioned the plan's underlying assumptions and predicted shortfalls of as much as 50%.[12] For both defence and budget analysts, and for many of America's allies, the conclusion was the same – US efforts to play the role of a regional balancer 'on the cheap' would clearly fail. Nor did the administration make it clear to the US public or to friends and allies in Asia what it hoped to achieve by its continued presence in the Asian theatre. President George Bush did not succeed in articulating a vision of US interests in Asia, and in the absence of such a vision Asian states were uneasy about the long-term reliability of the US commitment to the region.

The Clinton Administration
Candidate Bill Clinton argued during his 1992 presidential campaign that the major task for US policy in the Asia-Pacific was to 'form a broad consensus on how to reduce regional tensions and contain threats to regional security'.[13] Such statements generated interest and support among Asian commentators. Following Clinton's election, however, concerns quickly developed throughout the region about policy drift in America's Asia-Pacific strategy. In early 1994, Secretary of State Warren Christopher claimed that the United States did not require an 'overarching theme' to confront post-Cold War international security problems. By contrast, the Assistant Secretary of State for East Asia and the Pacific, Winston Lord, postulated a more activist approach and, during his confirmation hearings, outlined 'ten major goals' for US policy in the Asia-Pacific. Among these were strengthening ties with Japan; helping to resolve the Korean dispute; deepening ties with the Association of South-East Asian Nations (ASEAN); strengthening the Asia-Pacific Economic Cooperation group (APEC); and developing multilateral fora for security cooperation.[14] Unfortunately, Lord's criteria were too diffuse and too much at odds with each other to serve

as a basis for US policy. The 'promotion of human rights in China and Vietnam', for example, potentially contradicted the expressed need to 'restore firm foundations for cooperation with China' and 'normalise economic and diplomatic relations with Hanoi'. Nor was it clear how the 'developing of multilateral fora for security consultations' could be reconciled with 'maintaining the foundations' of the US bilateral security network in the region. Some Asian commentators began to draw parallels between Clinton's foreign-policy ambiguities and the contradictory pronouncements of the last Democratic administration, that of Jimmy Carter, in the late 1970s.[15]

The Clinton administration's espousal of the doctrine of 'enlargement' in late 1993 generated particular concern among Asia-Pacific states. The doctrine was most clearly articulated by Anthony Lake, Clinton's National Security Adviser, who defined enlargement as expanding 'the community of market democracies' by increasing their strength and numbers. This could be done, he argued, through four basic programmes:

- strengthening the 'core community' of market democracies through America's own economic revitalisation and that of its traditional economic allies;
- promoting democracy and market liberalisation 'beyond the core', particularly in the former Soviet Union, but also in Asia, Africa and Latin America;
- minimising the threat posed by 'backlash' states that resist democratic reforms with authoritarian and anti-liberal policies;
- pursuing a 'humanitarian agenda' that would include selective peacekeeping operations, disaster relief and related missions.[16]

At a time when key Asia-Pacific states are increasingly asserting their sovereignty, the 'Clinton doctrine' of enlargement has been widely interpreted as a campaign of interference and cultural imperialism. But the policy of enlargement did much more than offend the sensibilities of some Asia-Pacific states; it undermined the United States' ability to improve its bilateral relations with important regional actors – China in particular – during a crucial period in the post-Cold War era.

The Clinton administration has since coined the term 'engagement' to describe US attempts to adapt the concept of enlargement to its strategic and military planning. In early 1994, Chairman of the Joint Chiefs of Staff, General John Shalikashvili, stated that the strategy of engagement comprised the *prevention* of major threats to regional stability and *partnership* with friends and allies to help them take greater responsibility for peace and stability in their own regions. Like the EASI doctrine that preceded it, however, its core assumption about the Asia-Pacific region was the preservation of the basic elements of the San Francisco system.[17]

Admiral Charles Larson, Commander-in-Chief of the US Pacific Command, had already adapted the concept of engagement to circumstances in the Asia-Pacific. Using the term 'co-operative engagement', Larson envisioned applying US military resources for three purposes in the Asia-Pacific: to maintain a constant forward presence in the region; to reinforce regional alliances; and to achieve effective crisis-response capabilities.[18] Larson's use of the term 'engagement' to describe his own strategic outlook may have flowed from an extensive and influential 1992 RAND Corporation study, *A New Strategy and Fewer Forces: The Pacific Dimension*, which recommended that the US adopt a 'proportional engagement' posture.[19] Both Larson's and RAND's approaches, however, anticipated little more than holding fast to existing bilateral alliances and related security arrangements in the face of strategic uncertainty.

THE *BOTTOM-UP REVIEW*
Complementing the enlargement and engagement concepts was a Defense Department review of the overall US strategic posture – the *Bottom-Up Review*.[20] The study, initially introduced in September 1993, was foreshadowed by President Clinton's election promise to realise substantial reductions in defence spending. Prior to the election, Clinton's first Secretary of Defense, Les Aspin, had estimated that the defence budget could be slashed by $100 billion. The *Bottom-Up Review* was designed to meet that objective. In presenting it, Aspin cited nuclear proliferation, regional conflicts, the failure of international democratic reform and the erosion of economic well-being as the primary threats to US national security.

The *Bottom-Up Review* de-emphasised forward presence and sea control and placed more importance on rapid-force deployment and mobile amphibious combat capabilities to quell regional crises and conflicts (Table 3). The new posture foresaw the United States fighting and winning two regional conflicts (the Persian Gulf and Korean peninsula were cited as examples) 'nearly simultaneously' as part of an overall strategy of 'prevention and partnership'. Initially, Aspin termed this approach a 'win-hold-win' strategy because it called for US forces to hold the line against one adversary while defeating a second in another region.

Table 3: Major Regional Force Options in the *Bottom-Up Review*

Strategy	Win one major regional conflict	Win one major regional conflict; hold in second	Win in two near-simultaneous major regional conflicts (Pentagon's selected option)	Win in two near-simultaneous major regional conflicts plus additional duties
Army	8 active divisions 6 reserve division equivalents	10 active divisions 6 reserve division equivalents	10 active divisions 15 reserve enhanced readiness brigades	12 active divisions 8 reserve division equivalents
Navy	8 carrier battlegroups	10 carrier battlegroups 1 reserve/training carrier	11 carrier battlegroups	12 carrier battlegroups
Marine Corps	5 active brigades 1 reserve division	5 active brigades 1 reserve division	5 active brigades 1 reserve division	5 active brigades 1 reserve division
Air Force	10 active fighter 6 reserve fighter wings	13 active fighter wings 7 reserve fighter wings	13 active fighter wings 7 reserve fighter wings force enhancements	14 active fighter wings 10 reserve fighter wings

Source: Les Aspin, US Secretary of Defense, *The Bottom-Up Review: Forces For a New Era* (Washington DC: US Department of Defense, 1993), p. 11.

Analysts on both sides of the political spectrum in the US have been critical of the intellectual premises and strategic reasoning of the *Review*. Liberals, disappointed that the plan failed to deliver the deep spending cuts Clinton promised during his presidential campaign, complained that the *Review* trimmed the Base Force five-year plan by only about 7%, and treated post-Cold War regional threats as if they were as menacing to US security as the Soviet threat had been during the Cold War. They concluded that 'the Bush strategy was simply stuffed into the Clinton budget constraints' and, in fact, by the end of 1994, President Clinton had to request supplementary funds to get through the budget year. [21]

Not surprisingly, US conservatives expressed the opposite concerns. They argued that the administration had allowed a campaign commitment to budget cuts to determine the US strategic posture. They were highly sceptical that enough US military power would be available to fulfil the advertised mission of fighting and winning two medium-sized regional conflicts.[22] Even the authors of the *Review* admitted that setbacks in the C-17A military transport aircraft project (intended to strengthen US airlift capabilities by improving warning-time contingencies) rendered US force mobility questionable and that no alternative strategic-lift programme was likely to emerge in the near future.

At first the administration countered that two regional wars were unlikely to occur simultaneously because the Soviet Union no longer existed to project power throughout Eurasia. Then the Defense Department tried to quiet Congressional critics by elevating the strategy to the status of a 'win-win' doctrine. As many defence experts have since observed, however, Clinton's defence budget projections do not correspond to the demands of such a scenario.

With specific reference to the Asia-Pacific, the *Bottom-Up Review* argued that the effectiveness of the residual San Francisco system would be maintained by increasing US airlift capabilities, pre-positioning equipment near possible crisis spots, and stationing aircraft carriers and other surface ships in key locations. Economy of force would be realised by assigning primary responsibility for initial defence efforts to the allied country threatened or attacked. In North-east Asia, the Japanese and South Koreans would be expected to contribute more to the costs of a declining US military presence on their soil, in return for a US assurance that 'forces already in the theatre would move rapidly to provide assistance'.[23]

The Asia-Pacific theatre was less affected than Europe by the reductions in defence spending called for in the *Bottom-Up Review*.

According to the Center for Defense Information, US forces in Asia accounted for about $44bn (15% of the Clinton administration's proposed overall defence budget for fiscal year 1994).[24] Clinton administration officials emphasised that the *Review* dramatically reaffirmed the US commitment to maintaining a viable Pacific Command. They contended that 'within a few years there will be as many, if not more, American military personnel in the Asia-Pacific region as there are in Europe – about a hundred thousand'.[25]

In Asia, the *Bottom-Up Review* has nonetheless been regarded as part of a disturbing US tendency to reaffirm its traditional security commitments to the region while reducing its military power. Security analysts in South Korea, for example, have pointed out that the eight active US Army divisions that the Review stated would be maintained comprise about one-quarter of the personnel that the North Koreans currently field in their infantry, motorised and mechanised divisions.[26]

EASI-III

Sensing growing concern in Asia that the US military presence would be further reduced and that US willingness to become involved in regional security issues would be undercut by Congressional and public pressure, the Clinton administration released yet another version of EASI in February 1995.[27] The intended message of 'EASI-III' was that the US remained committed to a significant role in preserving regional stability. Its policy approach reflects what one US security analyst has characterised as a 'bridging or hedge' strategy: 'leaving open fuller responses in light of subsequent developments', but avoiding a full-fledged regional containment posture or an explicitly anti-China orientation.[28]

Yet, EASI-III varied little from existing US policy and reaffirmed the centrality of the San Francisco system. It failed to provide new conceptual tools to link post-Cold War US security interests with changing regional politico-strategic conditions. In particular, EASI-III equivocated between recommending that US bilateral alliances be strengthened as 'the heart' of US strategy for the region, and tacitly acknowledging the need for the United States to develop 'layers of multilateral ties' in Asia that would not erode the credibility of the existing US alliance system. Bilateral treaties, EASI-III argued, are more manageable than multilateral arrangements because 'the leading states in the Asia-Pacific region have diverse threat perceptions and disparate cultures, histories, political systems, and levels of economic development'.[29] Yet it presented no clear arguments to support the claim that bilateral defence pacts would be able to respond to regional threats more effectively than multilateral arrangements.[30]

Two additional problems undermine EASI-III's credibility. The document applied the term 'enlargement' in a vague context, to mean 'reaching beyond' the United States' traditional friends and allies in the region, without clarifying what was meant by reaching beyond, or addressing, building upon or revising the Clinton administration's original enlargement strategy. EASI-III also attempted to resurrect the *Bottom-Up Review* as a basis for Asia-Pacific security planning long after many Asian defence experts had criticised it.

The Clinton administration has been more explicit than its predecessor about the link between US foreign-policy goals and its regional defence plans. President Clinton is also less worried about how multilateralism might erode US regional influence. This helps to explain why many Asia-Pacific states were initially hopeful that the Clinton administration would be more willing than the Bush administration to confront the implications of change in the Asia-Pacific region. But Clinton's subsequent efforts to press the politics of enlargement upon Asian states, and his failure to articulate a coherent regional strategy, have made it hard for him to capitalise on this initially positive mood.

Why the San Francisco System Cannot Last
The American desire to maintain the San Francisco system of US-dominated bilateral alliances is certainly reasonable: why tinker with success? Those who favour preserving the Cold War system argue that the alliance network is still widely appreciated, or at least accepted, throughout the Asia-Pacific region. But while it is true that the San Francisco system still functions, it is rapidly approaching the end of its service life because of dramatic changes taking place in Asia, and fiscal and social problems that confront the United States domestically.

The Asian region is becoming too powerful to be either contained or controlled by the United States. This is most obvious in the economic realm. The Asia-Pacific has already become the new centre of gravity in the world economy and the most important variable in the United States' global economic calculus. APEC nations generate half the world's economic output, and, regardless of changes in the economic growth rates of specific Asian states, the region as a whole will continue to grow in importance within the global economy. Asian states are increasingly asserting their interests and are more willing to challenge US policies that affect the Asia-Pacific.

The United States faces an Asia that is also undergoing dramatic military change. Asian military modernisation programmes are largely attributable to the economic growth of the 1980s. While Asia-Pacific states may not actually be engaged in a region-wide arms race, the capabilities of their armed forces have nevertheless been dashing ahead – particularly in the areas of combined arms and maritime force projection. Over the next decade, as Asian military modernisation programmes continue, relative US military pre-eminence will decline, placing a commensurately greater premium on multilateral conflict avoidance and power balancing as means of preserving regional order.

These trends point not only to the 'Asianisation of Asia', but also to the Asianisation of world politics in the twenty-first century, as more of the decisions that affect global order are taken by Asian states.[31] The challenge for US foreign policy will be not only to adapt to change in the Asia-Pacific, but to help regional states to establish a place for Asia within the international system.

While the Asia-Pacific region as a whole is becoming more powerful and influential, China and Japan specifically are becoming world powers, whether they want to be (China) or not (Japan). Adjusting to the growth of Chinese power within Asia and in the wider global community is the most important foreign-policy issue facing the United States in the Asia-Pacific. The fact that it can only be accomplished in close cooperation with Japan further complicates US strategic calculations.

The most dramatic structural change that is likely to occur in the Asia-Pacific over the next decade is further progress towards North–South Korean unification. If Seoul and Pyongyang overcome their military stalemate in the next few years, it will be hard to imagine a future for the 36,000 US troops stationed in South Korea. Once this anchor of the San Francisco system disappears, the system itself will hardly be recognisable.

As US policy-makers cope with dramatic change in the Asia-Pacific, they are attempting to adjust to post-Cold War developments at home. The US Congress and electorate have become increasingly sensitive to indicators of relative US decline in the world, and increasingly isolationist regarding US global responsibilities. One US expert on Asia had this public mood in mind when he observed that 'in major part the threat [to Asian security] is within our own society'.[32]

The Clinton administration's 'gloves off' approach to US–Japan trade relations has played to nationalist instincts in US politics. This approach, however, has undermined the prospects for a new strategic dialogue between Washington and Tokyo that is so essential for the future of Asia-Pacific security. Notwithstanding the Clinton administration's persistent claims that the US–Japan security partnership is unaffected by ongoing economic disputes, the reality is very different. Indeed, both the United States and Japan seemed anxious to use the recent US threat of a 100% tariff on Japanese luxury cars as a pretext for a showdown on trade, and both sides were willing to hint at damage to the bilateral security relationship as a means of acquiring leverage in negotiations. Unless both states manage such disagreements more carefully in the future, they could precipitate the unravelling of the Mutual Security Treaty.

The MST is also vulnerable to other problems, as illustrated by the dispute over the future of US bases in Okinawa. Following the October 1995 arrest of three US servicemen stationed on the island on charges of rape, the Governor of Okinawa, Masahide Ota, announced that he opposed renewing the leases on land used for US military bases in Okinawa. Since 75% of the US Japan-based contingent is located on the island, the issue has significant implications for US strategy in Asia. In the past, US presidents could assume that such an incident would not escalate into a bilateral crisis. But this is no longer the case; a poll taken in the wake of the late 1995 Okinawa incident indicates that 40.2% of Japanese respondents now feel that the MST should be abolished, while only 43.5% still feel that the Treaty should be preserved.[33]

The San Francisco system was established at the end of the Second World War as a static system designed to send an unmistakably deterrent message to an identified enemy. There is no comparable unifying threat in post-Cold War Asia. Without such a threat it will be very difficult to articulate a coherent military rationale for preserving the system. US policy-makers will undoubtedly continue to justify the San Francisco framework by presenting it as an all-purpose, omni-directional deterrence blanket, but critics will continue to ask the question posed to George Bush when he warned of 'instability' in Europe at the end of the Cold War: 'how many divisions does instability have?'. Unlike in Western European, however, US leaders will not be able to finesse this question by referring to institutionalised commitments in multilateral fora, like NATO, that compel the United States to continue to contribute its 'fair share' to a communal security arrangement. Nor will it be easy for

US policy-makers to counter criticism by arguing, as they can in the case of Europe, that they are contributing to the defence of common 'Western' liberal values.

Some US policy-makers may be tempted to respond to growing domestic pressure for US force reductions by becoming more explicit (or even alarmist) about the threats that particular Asian actors pose. But by itself, a North Korean 'bogeyman' will not be sufficient. To generate the requisite level of long-term public support, it would be necessary to demonise either China or Japan – or both. Such a policy is neither wise nor necessary, and risks becoming a self-fulfilling prophesy. But while there is no visible threat, and in an ever-less malleable Asia-Pacific, domestic criticism of US defence commitments in Asia is likely to grow, to the detriment of America's military capability and regional influence.

II. BEYOND THE SAN FRANCISCO SYSTEM

It is likely that key elements of the current US alliance network in the Asia-Pacific will erode over the next decade. Consequently, the United States should prepare for this eventuality by encouraging the development of a new Asian security framework to protect its vital regional interests in the future. These vital interests are security and prosperity; the United States also recognises as an important interest the preservation and advancement of liberal values. Over the next decade, however, the United States will need to advance this important interest without jeopardising its vital interests.

Security
The United States in the mid-1990s is more secure from external military attack than it has been for four decades. It is unlikely, for at least the next decade, that Americans will face a direct military threat. The United States nonetheless needs to accord top priority to neutralising the one remaining (and admittedly distal) threat to its national survival – a direct strategic nuclear attack. The broad policy implications for the Asia-Pacific region are fairly clear. The United States has a special interest in improving relations with Russia and China, the two countries capable of launching such an attack against it. These are also the two great powers that can threaten America's Asia-Pacific allies with a nuclear attack. Russia's nuclear forces in the Asian theatre are declining in number but are still formidable, comprising one-third of its total stockpile of land- and sea-based strategic systems, and up to 1,000 tactical nuclear warheads.[1] China's nuclear force posture is primarily geared for potential regional conflicts even though its limited inventory of full-range CSS-4 (DF-5) land-based intercontinental ballistic missiles and ballistic-missile submarines give it the capability to strike the continental United States. The ongoing nuclear modernisation programme of the People's Liberation Army (PLA) is designed to bolster both its regional threat capability and its ability to retaliate against a US or Russian nuclear attack. Beijing's long-term goal is to diversify its delivery systems and enhance its second-strike survivability so that it will not have to capitulate in the event of a threat from either the United States or Russia – even though both countries still have nuclear arsenals approximately ten times larger than China's.[2]

The Clinton administration hopes that Moscow will continue to collaborate with Washington on issues of arms control and nuclear proliferation and that Beijing will eventually be more cooperative regarding these issues. Since, however, strategies of diplomatic co-optation are always risky, the United States is continuing its research and development programmes in the areas of ballistic-missile defence and theatre missile defence, and is discussing ways for key Asia-Pacific allies, such as South Korea and Japan, to collaborate in such programmes. Seoul and Tokyo have already noted their interest in working with Washington to develop anti-missile systems under the auspices of the Global Protection Against Limited Strikes (GPALS) programme.

The United States' long-term interest in reducing its strategic vulnerability also influences thinking about horizontal nuclear proliferation and the spread of missile technology. Once again, the centrality of China and Russia is clear: as the two nations with the greatest potential either for working with the US to control nuclear proliferation or for undermining the nuclear control regime, China and Russia must have top priority in American calculations. But the US would also be well advised to rely on other important Asian states and institutions to exert pressure on and create inducements for Beijing and Moscow. Japan's status – that of an economic powerhouse, a key US ally and a nation that formally eschews the acquisition of nuclear weapons and the development of an offensive military capability – makes it a uniquely important partner for the United States in this regard. South Korea's interests and insights also need to be taken into account, since it has the greatest stake in the peaceful management of the region's most threatening nuclear issue: North Korea's interest in acquiring a nuclear war-fighting capability.

As the world's only superpower, the United States also has an overriding interest in avoiding a major war in any region. The United States learned in 1917 and 1941 that it is simply too large and too globally integrated to isolate itself from any military struggle for regional hegemony. This consideration also highlights the importance of China in US foreign-policy plans for the Asia-Pacific. China will be the most influential actor in the region by the twenty-first century, as well as the nation most likely to precipitate a major regional war. Arguably, the most straightforward way for the US to prepare for this possibility would be to block the growth of Chinese politico-strategic influence. But this option is already untenable, and will become more so over the next several years. Aside from the risk of creating a self-fulfilling prophesy, it is also doubtful that either the US public or Beijing's neighbours would support such a containment posture. It would be equally misguided for the United States to commit itself overtly or covertly to encouraging fissiparous tendencies in China as a way of weakening or destroying the People's Republic.

If the United States can neither contain China nor engineer its collapse, US national security is best served by policies designed to enhance China's interest in cooperating with other Asia-Pacific states. But the United States cannot accomplish this alone; while focusing its attention on China, it will need to work more closely than in the past with other regional actors. In particular, the United States will need to reassure its two principal allies in North-east Asia – Japan and South Korea – of its continued commitment to their security, while pressing them to share in sponsoring a new multipolar Asia-Pacific security framework. US policy-makers will also need to support ASEAN's incremental approach to multilateral security cooperation in South-east Asia while preserving US military access to the sub-region.

Prosperity
Economics will also play a determining role in the Asia-Pacific security environment. There is considerable disagreement, however, about whether economics will encourage peace or lead to conflict in the region. One reason why this debate is hard to resolve is that the Asian economic milieu is a unique mixture of actors including national governments, multinational corporations, inter-governmental organisations and non-governmental organisations (NGOs).

The development of the APEC forum demonstrates the complex interaction of these economic actors. APEC was created in 1989 in response to the region's rapid and substantial economic growth in the 1980s which exacerbated local trade tensions and heightened competition for comparative advantage. Existing NGOs, like the Pacific Economic Cooperation Council (PECC), had already gone some way towards trust-building and identifying common economic interests throughout the region. The Asia-Pacific élite and policy analysts agreed, however, that something more was needed if they were to influence the global, GATT-based trading system on which their national economies increasingly depended. Regional multinational corporations also pushed for more systematic guidance from Asian states regarding such issues as infrastructure management, trade flows, information and technology exchange, and the movement of labour and capital. APEC was the institutional answer to these demands. Its stated purpose is to facilitate, rather than manage, intra-regional trade and investment. It is flexible, inclusive and compatible with the long-term goal of globalised free trade.

Regional organisations like APEC need to remain flexible in order to develop along with the rapidly expanding Asian regional economy. One analyst has highlighted the significance of the Asian growth 'tidal wave' as follows:

> This year [1994], the total GDP [gross domestic product], in real purchasing-power terms, of the 2.5 billion people in China, India, Japan and the Asian rim is probably about half that of the 800m in Europe and North America. By 2025, the Asian GDP will be double the Euro-American.[3]

The Asian regional economy is growing in size, and is also changing shape as the relative economic weight of various Asian countries rise and decline and as the balance between national and transnational economic forces undergoes constant adjustment.

The case of China is illustrative. Beijing has attempted to maintain control over its growing and changing economy, and transform its economic power into political influence. Yet China's leadership has frequently been frustrated by the forces of economic interdependence, which many Chinese policy-makers see as a threat to both national cohesion and self-reliance. The Chinese leadership understands that its survival depends on its ability to control the more dynamic elements of the economy while placating the sectors that are being left behind as the PRC 'changes shape'.[4] Resource distribution and economic development must expand from the coastal areas experiencing the greatest economic growth to the country's hinterland, which is lagging far behind. Closing the gaps between the richer coastal regions and the disadvantaged interior is made more difficult, however, by a slowly growing real per capita output in China (currently around $1,000 per annum) and by Beijing's need to increase imports of both capital goods and foodstuffs during the next few years.[5] China will need the help of its regional economic partners to manage a 'soft landing' – an economic adjustment that does not trigger uncontrollable inflation or lead to crippling budget deficits.[6] For their part, other Asian states recognise that they have a stake in China's continued economic success, even if they are unsure of Beijing's long-term political intentions.

Most Asian states also recognise that they have a common interest in economic cooperation with the United States. Yet the problem for US policy-makers is that this perspective is attributable in large part to the growth of Asian trade surpluses with the United States.

According to one expert, 'if the American market stopped being able to absorb so many Asian products, every country in the region would have to rethink its economic plans'.[7] The disappearance of the Soviet military threat has made it both possible and necessary for the US to focus more of its attention on the problem of US trade imbalances and, more broadly, on what President Clinton has called 'economic security'. In the Asia-Pacific region this interest is defined in terms of unimpeded US access to regional markets and Asian acceptance of the rules of the global free-trade regime. The challenge for the United States is to pursue this fundamental interest without alienating its best friends in the Asia-Pacific and undermining US national security and regional security.

The United States' relationship with Japan is at the core of this problem. Tokyo has the dubious distinction of being singled out by the Clinton administration as the most serious threat to US economic competitiveness. The United States has opted for unilateral, quantitative measures, including threats of quotas and tariffs, to reduce the merchandise trade deficit with Japan. US Senator Bill Bradley, a supporter of the Clinton administration on most issues, has called this approach 'gratuitous brinkmanship ... without regard to the long-term strategic interests of the United States'.[8]

The US–Japan trade dispute is the point at which US interests in security and prosperity most clearly intersect, for both interests would be best served by a new partnership to lay the groundwork for a multipolar regional order. During the Cold War, economics and military security were compartmentalised, and the latter was accorded top priority. In the post-Cold War era, priories have been reversed and economics and security have begun to be linked. However, linkage is being used for the wrong reason – as a means to acquire negotiating advantage in bilateral confrontations over trade.

There is also a growing tendency among Asia-Pacific states to take Japan's side in this dispute. These states fear that the US is abandoning its tradition of support for multilateral dispute settlement and that the coercive strategies it currently employs against Japan will be applied in the future against other nations in the region. Asian states have concluded that earlier concerns about the danger of a new Japanese-dominated 'Co-Prosperity Sphere' in the Asia-Pacific were unwarranted. Indeed, many Asian policy-makers now accept the need for a healthy Japanese economy, not only as an engine for regional economic growth, but also as a key component of a strong Asian front against an increasingly assertive United States. This is a particularly dangerous trend, for it threatens to drive a wedge between the United States and its regional friends and allies, when they should be developing new security cooperation practices in the Asia-Pacific.

Values
The end of the Cold War was a victory for liberal values. Not surprisingly, then, many American commentators have called upon US policy-makers to take advantage of the momentum provided by the end of the Cold War to 'fulfil America's destiny' as the source and model for a liberal and democratic world.[9] The Clinton administration took up this challenge by making the doctrine of enlargement the hallmark of its foreign policy. But within a year of announcing the doctrine, the administration had come to appreciate just how problematic the concept is as a policy guide.

The concept of enlargement assumes the pre-eminence of the individual in any theory of human rights. It thus adopts a literal interpretation of the 1966 International Covenant of Civil and Political Rights and seeks to apply these standards in its relations with Asian states. The argument for enlargement in Asia is guided by two other assumptions as well: that by pressing its version of human rights throughout the Asia-Pacific, the US is serving the interests of regional order, since the Asia-Pacific will be more peaceful and stable once it is composed of governments committed to civil and political rights; and, that there is no conflict between the advancement of individual liberty and the pursuit of economic prosperity in Asia, since market economies cannot progress indefinitely unless reinforced by political pluralism and civil liberties.[10]

Most Asia-Pacific states are at least sceptical of the notion that individual rights are superior to a society's collective interests. They are also uncomfortable with the assumption that the Western form of democracy is a superior form of governance. These societies are more likely to value state sovereignty, the preservation of domestic order and the priority of economic prosperity, and are more willing to defend publicly these different points of view than was the case just a decade ago. Furthermore, Asian leaders generally agree that democratisation must follow economic modernisation, rather than precede it or evolve concurrently to it.

Over the next few years, disputes between the United States and various Asian states over human rights could seriously undermine US security interests in the region. Most Asia-Pacific policy-makers support a continued US military and economic presence, and they are genuinely puzzled by what they see as the US tendency to jeopardise these common interests in the name of the West's conception of human rights. Some even see the enlargement strategy as economically confrontational, and as a ploy to rationalise a declining US force presence.[11] The depth of US–Asian misunderstanding on this issue became apparent when a US citizen was found guilty of vandalism by a Singapore court and sentenced to be caned. According to two Western commentators, 'the public spectacle of the United States repeatedly rebuking Singapore for its own law – hitherto unnoticed as a human rights violation when only Asians were caned' was an exercise in hypocrisy.[12] Many Asian leaders shared the interpretation that the incident was a sign of a US double standard in Asia.[13]

Since President Clinton's decision in May 1994 to 'de-link' China's human-rights record from issues of trade and diplomatic cooperation, the policy of enlargement has been less a source of disagreement between the US and other Asia-Pacific states. There is some concern, however, that this change has more to do with the fact that the Clinton administration has been distracted by issues like Haiti and Bosnia than with any fundamental reassessment of US priorities in Asia. Such suspicions can only be assuaged by an ongoing US–Asian dialogue on human rights. Any such dialogue should begin from the premise that US and Asian values are not irreconcilable, and that all of the societies in this dynamic region can benefit from the constructive integration of US idealism and Asian pragmatism.

Towards Moderate Multipolar Balancing
The best context for the protection of US interests in twenty-first century Asia is a moderate multipolar balance-of-power system. The challenge for US foreign policy-makers will be to encourage those trends that will lead to a benign and predictable balance of power, based on a common regional interest in avoiding a major war and a collective stake in continued economic growth.

The United States will face significant problems in working with other regional powers to establish such a system in the Asia-Pacific. Disagreements over the degree to which the United States should become involved in local territorial disputes, its proper role in regional 'trust-building' initiatives and its handling of bilateral economic disputes are just a few of the problems the United States is likely to confront.

III. US SECURITY: INTERESTS AND CHALLENGES

If a system of moderate multipolar balancing is to be established in the Asia-Pacific, the United States will need to work with other key regional states to resolve outstanding security problems in three places: on the Korean peninsula; across the Taiwan Strait; and in the South China Sea. The US will also have to reconcile its economic interests in the Asia-Pacific with its commitment to regional security goals.

South Korea and Taiwan are residual components of the San Francisco system, but the factors that shape their present security postures are very different from those that were operative in the 1950s. US foreign policy must help to preserve stability on the Korean peninsula and across the Taiwan Strait, while contributing to positive change in both regions. The dispute in the South China Sea involves conflicting territorial claims by six regional states and engages the interests of several more. US policy-makers will have to adjust to the growth of Chinese power in this region, while establishing a new cooperative relationship with the nations of South-east Asia. Meanwhile, trade issues are complicating relations among Asia-Pacific states with otherwise complementary security interests. The United States will need to protect its economic interests in Asia without undermining either the system of global economic cooperation it sponsored during the Cold War, or the new system of security cooperation essential for regional order in the twenty-first century.

The Korean Peninsula
The intensification of the North Korean nuclear crisis and the death of North Korea's leader Kim Il Sung in mid-1994 reinforced the belief already firmly held in Washington that North Korea is one of the two most immediate threats (along with Iraq) to the 'new world order'. US and South Korean forces confront a North Korean military – the world's fourth largest at more than one million personnel – poised to initiate a massive offensive operation against them. At the same time, the very survival of North Korea is in doubt due to its shattered economy, international isolation and problems associated with the efforts of North Korea's new leader, Kim Jong Il, to perpetuate his late father's 'cult of personality' – the basis for the regime's political legitimacy. In the face of these uncertainties, US policy towards the Korean peninsula is guided by three clear interests:

- sustaining a viable deterrent in order to avoid war on the peninsula;
- facilitating the peaceful reunification of North and South Korea without alienating South Korea in the process;

- and ensuring that a unified Korea plays a constructive role in any future regional power balance.

Deterrence and War Avoidance

Deterring war on the Korean peninsula is the most critical short-term US security interest in the region. Until unification of the Democratic People's Republic of Korea (DPRK) to the north and the Republic of Korea (ROK) in the south is accomplished, the risk of conflict on the peninsula is likely to increase as North Korea's communist regime struggles to maintain its ideological legitimacy and overcome a deteriorating economy. A new Korean conflict would cause substantial casualties among both South Korean and US forces, increase the risk of direct Sino-American military confrontation in North-east Asia, and pose a direct threat to Japan.

To contribute to war avoidance in a divided Korea, two problems will need to be addressed. One concerns North Korea's nuclear status, the related issue of its ballistic-missile capabilities, and the fulfilment of the terms of the US–North Korean Agreed Framework to prevent the DPRK from producing nuclear weapons. The Agreed Framework can then serve as a precedent for other trust-building measures on the peninsula. Second, the Clinton administration and its successors will need to respond more effectively to criticisms that the US–South Korea Mutual Defence Treaty is outdated.

The history of North Korea's nuclear-weapons programme has been assessed extensively. Less attention has been directed to how a North Korean nuclear force would actually affect US strategic interests and planning in North-east Asia. Certainly, the US and South Korea would have to revise their existing military strategies against the North, which reportedly still focus on the threat of a non-nuclear ground attack by North Korean forces into South Korea and upon a substantial US–ROK counter-attack into North Korea's heartland (as embodied in the US Forces' Operational Plan 5027). North Korean nuclear warheads deployed on *Scud* missiles would give the DPRK considerable leverage by simultaneously threatening South Korean airfields and air command-and-control centres, population centres and economic infrastructure. Such a force would provide Pyongyang with the means to bargain for a 'troops-in-place' settlement after its forces had occupied portions of ROK territory through a *blitzkrieg* attack.[1]

US deterrence calculations beyond the peninsula would also be affected. One analyst has observed that North Korea's enlargement of its 'strategic space' – by its deployment of *No-dong* ballistic

Clinton administration officials have not made a concerted effort to refute these arguments, preferring to reiterate that the US must continue to honour its regional alliance commitments. Sufficient during the Cold War, this argument may not be adequate for the next few years. A more active approach would entail making the case at home and abroad that US forces contribute to stability on the Korean peninsula, and throughout the entire North-east Asian region, at a time when the two Korean adversaries are moving haltingly towards reunification.

The military rationale for maintaining US forces in South Korea is fairly straightforward. According to the *Strategic Assessment 1995* published by the US National Defense University:

> The Republic of Korea Army has begun to address historical problems related to intelligence, command and control, air defence, and air and naval capabilities. Scheduled improvements ... will eventually help to remove remaining weaknesses ... In the short term, however, US assistance will continue to be necessary.[8]

There is also an economic rationale for a continued US troop commitment to Korea. Much of South Korea's current leverage over (and appeal to) the North is the result of substantial economic growth made possible in part by the US security connection that has enabled successive South Korean governments to spend less on defence than would otherwise have been necessary. The challenge for US policy-planners is to convince the US Congress and electorate of the Korean peninsula's importance for the strategic calculations of both China and Japan, and its consequent importance for US national security.

Korean Re-Unification
Along with deterrence and war avoidance on the peninsula, the establishment of a unified, pro-American, democratic and non-nuclear Korea constitutes a second critical US interest in North-east Asia. This involves working with Seoul to achieve the peaceful transformation of North Korea.

North Korea's economic vulnerability and growing political isolation is a unique variant of the 'stability–instability paradox' used to explain the logic of brinkmanship.[9] In this case, all parties have an interest not only in avoiding war (the standard brinkmanship scenario), but also in avoiding the implosion of the North Korean regime. And since the latter outcome is the more likely, it is the one that affords the North Korean regime the most leverage. If Kim fails to stem the tide of economic decay and political decline in North Korea, a rapid and uncontrolled collapse of the regime could trigger an unprecedented political and economic crisis in South Korea.

Even if reunification is carefully managed by both North and South Korea, the process is likely to present the United States with new political problems. As the pace of North–South reconciliation accelerates, the future of a US military presence will become an important element of the negotiations, particularly if the two Koreas use the 1991 Basic Agreement on Reconciliation, Non-Aggression and Exchange-Cooperation as a basis for discussion. If the United States is then perceived as a barrier to unification, the vague sense of discomfort South Koreans feel regarding the US protectorate will begin to assume form and content. In these circumstances, managing domestic anti-Americanism could become as much a problem for Seoul as managing the unification process.

US–South Korean relations could become even more complicated if the two nations permit their economic disputes to affect diplomatic and security relations. At present, South Korea is experiencing all the problems of a mature economy – a relative decline in regional competitiveness, increasing demands for higher wages and a growing current account deficit (which in 1995 is set to more than double 1994's deficit of $4.8bn).[10] These economic concerns have tended to exacerbate outstanding problems in US–South Korean economic relations, largely generated by US pressure on South Korea to lower trade barriers on cars, food and telecommunications products.

Korea in the Region
The United States will also need to work with the South Korean government to keep China, Japan and Russia involved in and supportive of Korean unification. At present, this does not seem to be a problem, but the situation could change rapidly if the pace of peninsular talks accelerates and China, Russia and Japan have to accommodate another major regional power.

In fact, South Korea has already begun to exercise considerable diplomatic and economic influence in the Asia-Pacific region. South Korea's 'Northern Diplomacy' reaped its greatest rewards with the normalisation of relations with the USSR in September 1990 and with China in August 1992: the South Koreans were able to convince Russia and China to decouple diplomatic and economic policy from security commitments to North Korea. South Korean President Kim Young Sam has also revived annual South Korean–Japanese Foreign Ministers meetings (briefly discontinued in 1992) and has acted to reduce tariffs on a wide range of Japanese imports. In return, Japanese Prime Minister Hosokawa Morihiro publicly apologised for his country's history of colonialism in Korea during a November 1993 meeting with Kim in Kyongju. Both South Korea and Japan, however, must avoid undercutting improved relations by preventing their politicians from hurling invectives about the other country's role in the Second World War.[11]

Such positive diplomatic initiatives are part of President Kim's campaign for the 'globalisation' of South Korean foreign policy, designed to 'enhance the nation's international status and actively contribute to the shaping of a new world order'.[12] It is worth noting that the South Korean government undertook this campaign fully confident of US support and protection were it to prove unsuccessful. The United States would be well advised to continue to support the South's new activism in foreign affairs since the interests of the two are fundamentally compatible. An ambitious South Korean foreign policy also helps to prepare North-east Asian states for the time when they will need to find a place in their midst for a unified Korea with 68m citizens and a military force of perhaps one million well-armed troops.

China–Taiwan

As China has not yet decided what to do with its new geopolitical, economic and military power in the Asia-Pacific, the United States now has a vital national interest in helping to convince China to play a cooperative and constructive role in the region. This can only be accomplished if the US is consistent and firm in its policies towards the PRC. Yet even members of the Clinton administration have reportedly admitted that its policy in the Asia-Pacific has been *ad hoc*, reactive and driven by short-term considerations.[13] US policy towards China, guided by the wrong priorities and pursued with the wrong tactics, has been especially problematic. The risks inherent in US ambivalence are especially clear with regard to the issue of Taiwan.

China's relations with Taiwan are emerging as a critical test of Beijing's intentions in the Asia-Pacific. The PRC has become increasingly bellicose in its actions towards Taiwan and in its statements on issues relating to reunification. According to the Chinese government, Taiwan remains part of China, and its future must be resolved by the People's Republic alone. From the US perspective, the issue is not that simple; the US still adheres to the 'one China' principle as stipulated in the 1972 Shanghai Communiqué, but successive US governments have also maintained a distinct and enduring set of interests regarding Taiwan. Taiwan – strategically situated along the Taiwan Strait and Bashi Channel – is a gateway into both North-east and South-east Asia and is a potential base for future US military operations in a regional or global crisis. As the world's third largest foreign investor (after Germany and Japan) and one of the world's most competitive trading economies (ranking twelfth as an exporter and seventeenth as an importer in 1991, in dollar-denominated trade volume), Taiwan is already an important source of stability and prosperity.[14] Taiwan has also become a model for how the US believes 'Asian democracies' should develop: integrating capitalism and democratisation by converting the rising expectations of a growing middle class into a genuinely pluralistic national political infrastructure.[15] As a result, Taiwan has attracted the attention and support of numerous US business interests, cultural groups and, increasingly, the US Congress.

The United States opposes any use of force by China to re-acquire Taiwan. Indeed, the Taiwan Relations Act (TRA) of 1979 actually goes much further by committing the US 'to maintain the capacity ... to resist any resort to force or other forms of coercion that would jeopardise the security or social or economic system, of the people on Taiwan'.[16] This official position was relatively easy to maintain as long as China–Taiwan relations were in a stalemate. The US stance has become more problematic in recent years, however, as Taiwan has begun to play a more visible international role and as the forces of national self-determination have assumed greater prominence on the island. Taiwanese President Lee Teng-hui's private visit to his US Alma Mater, Cornell University, in early June 1995 created problems for the United States, because Beijing strongly opposes any Taiwanese 'head of state' setting foot on US soil, much less speaking about Taiwan's democratic development to US audiences and meeting members of Congress. As one PRC commentator observed:

> By permitting [Lee] to visit the United States, Washington is brazenly supporting his attempt to create 'two Chinas' or 'one China, one Taiwan'. This cannot but arouse the vigilance of the Chinese people because the question of Taiwan bears on [their] national feelings.[17]

China responded to Lee's visit by recalling its ambassador from Washington; postponing a visit by its defence minister to the US; calling off talks with the United States relating to the Missile Technology Control Regime; suspending a scheduled round of cross-Strait negotiations; and intensifying PLA military exercises off the Zhejiang coast north of Taiwan. Furthermore, China's *Xinhua* news agency fuelled anti-Taiwan sentiments within China by warning that 'fresh blood and lives' would be the price of any Taiwanese attempt to block reunification with the Chinese mainland.[18]

Avoiding War in the Strait

The United States' most important interest with regard to Taiwan is clearly to avoid military confrontation across the Taiwan Strait. Any such conflict would force the US to choose between intervening on Taiwan's behalf and risking war with China, or failing to honour its long-standing pledge to defend Taiwan against Chinese aggression at the risk of irreparable damage to its strategic influence throughout the Asia-Pacific region. Hostilities are not likely to erupt in the Taiwan Strait as long as Taipei refrains from issuing a formal declaration of independence from China. The Taiwanese presidential election scheduled for 1996 could intensify the public debate over 'Taiwanisation', however, and put pressure on a post-Deng Xiaoping Chinese leadership to use force to reassimilate the island into the Chinese mainland. Influential US politicians, such as Speaker of the House of Representatives Newt Gingrich, could also encourage Beijing to gamble with using force if they continue to press for recognition of Taiwan as a *de facto* independent state. Gingrich commented in July 1995 that the United States should recognise Taiwan as 'a free and independent nation'. Although he subsequently backed down from the statement, his actions stand as a clear case of how *not* to protect US interests in the Taiwan Strait.[19]

China's current strategic planning assumes that limited war along its periphery now constitutes the greatest threat to its national security. This posture, in turn, represents the most pressing challenge to Taiwan's security. The PLA Navy (PLAN) is gradually improving its operational capabilities, including its ability to employ attack submarines and fast-attack craft to interdict shipping lanes along the Strait. Its recent purchase of several advanced *Kilo*-class diesel submarines from Russia should substantially improve the PLAN's ability to engage in mine-laying operations in and around the Taiwan Strait.[20] The PLAN has also added to its force inventories new *Luhu*-class destroyers and *Jiangwei*-class missile frigates with fire control systems, mine warfare ships and electronic countermeasures which will allow China to undertake naval operations at greater distances.[21]

Other elements of the People's Liberation Army are also being improved in ways that could threaten Taiwan. The PLA Air Force has now acquired Russian Su-27 jet fighters and is reportedly set to co-produce additional ones with Russia. These additions to China's air-combat power are designed to offset traditional Taiwanese air superiority and to counterbalance Taiwan's recent purchase of 150 US-supplied F-16A/B fighter aircraft and 60 French-built *Mirage 2000-5* multi-role aircraft. The Su-27s can also be used for long-range missions in the South China Sea and North-east Asia. In addition, PLA rapid-reaction units are being developed and trained to spearhead amphibious assaults in future combat supported by these upgraded naval and air units. The rapid-reaction units can also be used for internal security and border defence needs.[22]

Most Western and Taiwanese military analysts believe that Taiwan could not withstand a full-scale Chinese onslaught for more than three months without US military intervention. These observers are also convinced, however, that the costs and risks to China of undertaking such an offensive are still prohibitive, and that there are still serious flaws in China's war-fighting capacity.[23] For example, air-strips and naval facilities in the Fujian province opposite Taiwan are still underdeveloped and vulnerable to Taiwanese counter-strikes in the event that China attempts an amphibious invasion of Taiwan. Chinese leaders must also take seriously the possibility that the United States will come to the aid of Taipei before the PLA has had time to wear down Taiwan's defences. While not representing official Chinese defence policy, a highly publicised 'neibu' (restricted and internally circulated) book written in 1993 by PLA naval officers, *Can China's Armed Forces Win the Next War?*, argues that a Chinese invasion of Taiwan could not succeed if US forces intervened on Taiwan's behalf.[24]

If, despite its military modernisation efforts, China is still deterred from invading across the Strait by Taiwan's military preparations and the risk of US military intervention, why should US policy-planners be concerned? The answer lies in a combination of factors. First, the pace and scope of China's military modernisation, and particularly its enhanced ability to purchase advanced weapons systems from Russia, may offset Taiwan's qualitative advantages in air superiority, naval fire control systems and anti-submarine warfare. The PLA is attempting, for example, to redress deficiencies in the Fujian district by deploying an artillery division equipped with M-9 surface-to-surface missiles there.[25] Second, China's growing second-strike nuclear capability against US targets could erode the US commitment to extended deterrence over the next decade. Third, further reductions in forward-deployed US forces in North-east

Asia might alter China's assessment of the risks involved in any future US intervention on behalf of Taiwan. And finally, even if rough parity persists in the China–Taiwan military balance, the danger of a strategic miscalculation could increase if the Chinese leadership is caught up in a post-Deng succession struggle.

The risks of crisis mismanagement will only increase if the PRC continues to rely on its military forces to intimidate Taipei. The most serious recent example of this behaviour occurred in July 1995 when Beijing conducted tests of surface-to-surface missiles only 140km north of Taiwan. The action prompted panic on the Taiwanese stock exchange and consternation among Taiwanese government officials. The tests were meant to communicate Chinese anger over Taiwan's efforts to upgrade its diplomatic ties with the West and its campaign for separate UN membership. Reports filtering out of Hong Kong attributed the action to the influence of PLA commanders who believe that the military option is now the best means of resolving the Taiwan issue.[26] The challenge for US policy-makers is to discourage such thinking within the Chinese leadership while reassuring Taipei and supporting trust-building measures across the Taiwan Strait.

Trust Building Across the Taiwan Strait

Policies designed to reassure Taipei and shore up the US deterrent message to Beijing must be carefully managed so as not to undermine trust-building and reconciliation efforts between China and Taiwan. Such efforts must be initiated by one of the disputants, Beijing or Taipei, while Washington plays a low-key supportive role. One positive development took place in May 1991 when Taiwan's Kuomintang government announced that it was ending the Period for the National Mobilisation for Suppression of the Communist Rebellion and revising its major security policy from that of recapturing the Chinese mainland to merely protecting Taiwan, the Pescadores, Kinmen and Matsu. Although China rejected Taiwan's subsequent proposal for a non-aggression agreement that would have required Beijing's leaders to renounce the use of force as an option for re-assimilating Taiwan into China, Taiwan's suspension of its technical state of war with China was a significant confidence-building development. Since the end of the Cold War, there has also been a steady growth in economic and social ties across the Taiwan Strait. Two-way trade between China and Taiwan amounted to $16bn in 1994, Taiwanese citizens have invested more than $15bn on the mainland, and approximately 2.5m Taiwanese tourists visit the PRC each year.[27]

These positive trends are likely to continue as long as China remains confident that reunification with Taiwan will eventually occur without the use of force. The notion of the Chinese Communist Party and Taiwan's Kuomintang vying for the loyalty of one great Chinese populace continues to be unpalatable to the Beijing leadership, but Beijing has been careful to avoid a cross-Strait war. Nevertheless, China has consistently and stridently asserted that any attempt to establish 'two Chinas' or 'one China and one Taiwan' would demand military action. Any perceived or actual US effort to facilitate Taiwanese independence would inflame Chinese nationalism and rekindle fears in Beijing that foreigners were once again attempting to subjugate China and to deprive it of its proper international status. Moreover, Taiwanese separatism is likely to remain unacceptable to any future Chinese government regardless of its political make-up.

This requires the US to maintain a calculated distance from Taiwan. US support for a democratic and self-confident Taiwan needs to be weighed against the more important US interest in conflict avoidance across the Taiwan Strait. As one analyst has observed, US sympathy for the rights of native Taiwanese who wish to be free from China need to be measured against broader geopolitical calculations:

> The American people in principle favor the self-determination of peoples, but would not necessarily favor intervention by US armed forces to defend the right to self-determination of any ethnic group that chose to raise the banner of independence. US military intervention would be likely only in rare instances where, in addition to the defense of the principle of self-determination, vital US interests were involved.[28]

The South China Sea

America's collective memory of the Vietnam War and the attenuated US military presence in the region all but rules out direct US involvement in another South-east Asian conflict unless US lives and property are threatened. Yet the geostrategic importance of the South China Sea, situated in the critical maritime corridors between the Strait of Malacca and North-east Asia, is undeniable. If a hostile power gained control over the area it would be able to interdict much of Japan's imported oil and natural gas and disrupt US and allied naval and maritime operations in the region.[29] This helps to explain why the international community is so concerned about the ongoing dispute over the Spratly Islands, located in the southern part of the South China Sea. All or part of this grouping of approxi-

of the disputants. Since then, US statements have carefully avoided challenging China's territorial claims in South-east Asia. The United States has thus gradually become more active in the Spratlys dispute, while retaining the option to change its position if US security interests are affected.

Three of the four ASEAN claimants to the Spratlys (Brunei, Malaysia and the Philippines) have occasionally complained that the US refusal to take a stronger position with regard to the jurisdictional question is a *de facto* capitulation to pressure from both the Chinese and US oil firms that have offshore drilling contracts with China and Vietnam. Furthermore, the Philippines has expressed frustration over the US refusal to link the Philippines' territorial claims in the South China Sea to US obligations under the 1951 US–Philippines Mutual Defence Treaty.

The difficulty posed by US reluctance to play a more ambitious military or diplomatic role in the South China Sea is that there is no incentive or mechanism other than deterrence to constrain the Chinese from aggressively pursuing their own claims and interests there. ASEAN states have yet to develop anything resembling a common approach to defending the sub-region because they have failed to overcome their legacies of mutual suspicion, and they have little propensity to establish a joint military command. This situation will not change until the states concerned come to recognise a mutual stake in and collective responsibility for regional security. If such an attitude change is to take place among ASEAN states, it is likely to grow out of their already strong common interest in economic prosperity. US policy-makers need to encourage this sense of community among ASEAN states while continuing to oppose efforts to establish ASEAN as an exclusive and anti-American trading bloc.

Free Trade
In November 1994, 18 heads of state convened at the APEC forum in Bogor, Indonesia, and pledged to establish a free trade area for industrialised economies by the year 2010 and for developing economies by 2020. The Bogor Declaration reflected a growing realisation among Asia-Pacific states that their economic disputes could devolve into security conflicts if left unchecked. Two respected US economists have been more explicit concerning the risks:

> For the moment, Asia-Pacific tensions largely spring out of economic differences rather than ideological or territorial disputes ... [M]ore important than conflicting claims to the Spratly Islands are the challenges posed by Japan's persistent trade sur-

pluses, China's explosive growth as an exporter of manufactured goods, and exaggerated US concerns that trade with Asia will depress the wages of unskilled workers.[43]

All three of these challenges deserve discussion in terms of their impact on US security interests in the Asia-Pacific region.

Reconstructing the US–Japan Partnership

Japan's post-war strategy of promoting its own economic growth by expanding foreign markets and protecting its domestic industries has become a liability for the Japanese themselves and a source of frustration for Japan's principle trading partners. Now that the cornerstone of US–Japan post-war strategic collaboration – containment of global communism – has been removed, US public opinion is critical of the US role in underwriting the security of a country that has very low defence expenditure (approximately 1% of GDP) and is increasingly perceived as the greatest challenge to US economic competitiveness. In a February 1992 poll, 65% of US respondents reportedly believed anti-Japanese feelings were intensifying in the United States, and 63% said they were trying to avoid buying Japanese products.[44] Another poll conducted for the Japanese Foreign Ministry in early 1995 indicated that only 38% of US respondents held 'generally favourable' impressions of Japan.[45]

US policy-makers and 'opinion-makers' tend to hold more positive views of Japan. There is nevertheless growing concern within this community that US–Japan trade tensions and the political weakness of successive Japanese governments are eroding the US–Japanese security relationship. Following another round of bitter negotiations between the Clinton administration and the Murayama government on vehicle tariffs in late May 1995, Winston Lord warned that if the US public believed that the United States was being blocked from Asian markets, they might begin to question maintaining US forces in the Asia-Pacific.[46] A March 1995 US Congressional study drew a similar conclusion, arguing that the US would fast approach the time when economic tensions with Japan jeopardise bilateral defence cooperation unless new ways to separate trade questions from alliance politics are devised.[47]

The risk of a crisis in US–Japan relations is exacerbated by a new mood of assertive independence in Japan. In a post-Cold War environment where threats are more diffuse, a growing number of Japanese politicians are willing to challenge the United States on economic and political issues, even if such actions threaten the Mutual Security Treaty, the core of the US–Japan security partnership since 1951. Some Japanese commentators have also begun to question the cost of the existing host-nation support arrangements on the grounds that US forces in Japan are contributing not just to Japanese security but to deterrence on the Korean peninsula and to overall Asia-Pacific security as well. These arguments have had an effect on the Japanese government, which announced in April 1995 that it would reverse a policy in effect since 1958 of automatically increasing Japan's financial contributions to equal the cost of US forces stationed in the country. Whatever the outcome of the current round of Status of Forces Agreement (SOFA) negotiations, it seems clear that the United States can no longer take for granted that Japan will accept US terms and conditions relating to the MST. Indeed, the Japanese reaction to the Okinawa rape case illustrates that for a growing number of Japanese citizens the MST is no longer the 'only game in town'.

The dependence of the Japanese Self-Defense Forces (SDF) on and their collaboration with the US military has been a corner-stone of Asia-Pacific stability since the early days of the Cold War. Maintaining a viable US–Japanese security relationship in the face of growing bilateral tensions will be a critical challenge for both Washington and Tokyo for the foreseeable future. In particular, US and Japanese policy-makers will need to respond forcefully to nationalist constituencies in both countries that are willing to jeopardise the still indispensable Mutual Security Treaty to gain leverage in trade talks.

Assimilating China
The importance of protecting the US–Japan security relationship from the corrosive effects of economic and political disputes can only be appreciated against the backdrop of China's evolving power. Over the next decade, the United States and its regional allies will need to draw China into the institutions and cooperative practices of the liberal global economy. This will be an extremely difficult task, in part because US economic relations with China cannot be isolated from the complexities of state–society relations within the PRC. The forces of civil society are most highly developed, and therefore most threatening to the authority of the Chinese state, in the coastal areas where economic progress has been most dramatic. Beijing finds itself in a classic dependency relationship with these outward-looking provinces: frustrated by its lack of control over their activities and concerned about 'cultural pollution', it is also convinced of the indispensability of the coastal regions to China's

economic future. Any US economic initiatives towards China will need to be pursued in such a way that they are not interpreted by Beijing as *sub rosa* efforts to encourage China's fragmentation into rich and poor provinces.

Beijing's commitment to economic progress provides the best leverage the United States and its friends and allies have with China. In January 1995, the Japanese press reported that a joint research team of the Chinese Communist Party, the Chinese government and the PLA had circulated a document on China's post-Cold War security which assigned 'top priority' to China's economic construction.[48] Attracting foreign investment and expanding trade links with the developed world are essential to achieving this objective. Chinese policy-makers nonetheless remain apprehensive about any actions that increase China's economic involvement in the global economy, as such involvement is seen to be at odds with the traditional Chinese (and Maoist) emphasis on national self-reliance.

In spite of these concerns, the Chinese leadership remains committed to China's further integration into the global economy. A key element in this campaign is China's membership in the major multilateral institutions that oversee the world economy. The US recognises that it has an interest in supporting the principle of Chinese membership in such organisations, but only if China accepts the rules and purposes for which the organisations were created.

China's efforts to become a member of the World Trade Organization (WTO) has provided the US with its most important test to date. In 1994, the Chinese leadership pressed their case for founding membership in the WTO. The US delegation to the 1994 APEC summit made it clear, however, that while it was pleased by China's interest in the new organisation, the date of its entry would depend on greater progress towards full convertibility of its currency, reform of its intellectual property and copyright laws, and the removal of specific barriers to international trade. The Chinese reacted to such demands with expressions of outrage and defiance, but US policy-makers maintained a creditable, quiet resolve. In March 1995, an agreement was reached that addressed most of the US concerns and cleared the way for China to move forward with its application for WTO membership.

US handling of the Chinese request for WTO membership is a good example of how leverage can be applied to move China's decision-making in a positive direction. This leverage will not disappear once China becomes a member of the WTO. If managed properly, China can be encouraged to recognise a growing stake in cooperation with multilateral economic institutions and with the principles of free trade and rule-based dispute resolution. Even if Chinese leaders conclude that they are losing control over the economy (particularly in the more dynamic coastal regions), they will likely discover that they have no choice but to continue to participate in the WTO and other international economic institutions. This is why, as one analyst has observed, 'if it could see the future clearly, [China] might not want WTO membership'.[49]

Reconciling Regionalism with Globalism

A global system of rule-based free trade is an essential context for moderate multipolar balancing in Asia. As APEC's Eminent Persons Group has argued, if trade protectionism and trade blocs become the defining characteristics of the world economy, it could eventually generate intractable political and strategic conflicts along geographic or ethnic lines.[50] Restricted access to the Asia-Pacific trading economies would be especially damaging to the global trading system since Asia is the most dynamic region in the world economy. The Malaysian proposal for the creation of an exclusionary East Asian Economic Caucus (EAEC) poses these risks.

In keeping with its commitment to globalised free trade, the US will need to continue to resist protectionist trends in the Asia-Pacific that jeopardise US access to the region. President Clinton made this point during the APEC summits in Seattle (1993) and Bogor (1994). In Seattle, the President placed the North American Free Trade Agreement (NAFTA) in the larger context of the General Agreement on Tariffs and Trade (GATT) and assured Asian states that NAFTA would not develop into an exclusionary trading bloc. At the same time, Clinton made it clear that the US would actively oppose any efforts to create potentially anti-American groupings in Asia. With specific reference to the proposed EAEC, the President stated that the United States does 'not intend to bear the cost of [its] military presence in Asia, and the burdens of regional leadership, only to be shut out of the benefits of growth that that stability brings'.[51] The statement was entirely appropriate, both as a matter of principle and as a tactic for protecting US economic interests.

In the future, US presidents will need to continue sending strong messages to Asia-Pacific states, while resisting the forces of neo-mercantilism and neo-isolationism at home. This will not be an easy balance to maintain. The economies of East Asia are predicted to grow twice as fast as the US economy over the next decade, while intra-Asian trade is already growing four times faster than US–

Asian trade. In addition, the rapidly industrialising and post-industrial states of East Asia are among the world's worst exploiters of the liberal free trade regime. US policy-makers will need to cope with intense domestic resentment while seeking to compensate for the relative decline in US economic influence over Asian markets and states, all the while holding to its commitment to a rule-based free trade regime.

reconnaissance system (JSTARS) aircraft in South Korea prior to the outbreak of fighting.

Assessments vary as to how long it would take North Korean forces to break through South Korean and US defences, but most experts calculate it to be between two and four weeks. By this time, much of Seoul could already be decimated by North Korean rocket and artillery systems deployed close to the inter-Korean border. To deter North Korea from launching such an attack, or to minimise the damage if deterrence were to fail, US air-power and anti-missile systems would have to be available at the very beginning of a conflict. This would require immediate deployment of US carrier forces close to the combat area. To prepare for such a contingency, US defence planners would have to continue to deploy and train carrier assets in the seas immediately surrounding the peninsula.

This policy is not without diplomatic and military risks, as illustrated by the late 1994 confrontation in the Yellow Sea between the US carrier *Kitty Hawk* and a Chinese submarine. The US naval vessel had been despatched from Japan in June 1994 as a 'demonstrative deterrence' action at the height of the North Korean nuclear dispute. In October, the *Kitty Hawk* detected a PLA submarine within its operational area and launched sonobuoys and anti-submarine aircraft to track its movements. The Chinese responded by despatching jet fighters in the direction of the aircraft carrier. A military crisis was averted when the PLA submarine returned to its base at Qingdao, but Chinese officials warned the US that in future any such incident would justify orders to PLA aircraft to 'shoot to kill'.[3] The Chinese press treated the *Kitty Hawk* incident as 'a test for China in defending its maritime rights and interests'.[4]

The United States has an interest in establishing agreements with China designed to avoid such incidents at sea. But it should accept neither Beijing's definition of the situation, nor the implications of the Chinese argument. For the foreseeable future, the United States' alliance commitments to both South Korea and Japan will require a large and active maritime presence in North-east Asian waters, no matter how expansive China's sovereign claims are.

Contributing to Korean Re-unification
The US military presence on the Korean peninsula is likely to be substantially reduced, or totally eliminated, once there is significant progress towards Korean re-unification. But even if there is only modest and steady progress towards this goal over the next few years, the growing strength of both the South Korean military and

economy and the removal of the Soviet military threat in North-east Asia may render the continued deployment of 36,000 US troops on the Korean peninsula increasingly controversial in both the United States and South Korea.

Now that both Russia and China have downplayed their security commitments to Pyongyang and have improved trade ties with Seoul, the US cannot allow its forces on the peninsula to be viewed as a barrier to North–South reconciliation. To avoid this predicament, the US needs to help Seoul and Pyongyang strengthen trust-building measures on the peninsula without undermining the US–South Korean deterrence posture.[5] As a first step, the United States could actively encourage the implementation of measures included in the two Koreas' December 1991 Basic Agreement on Reconciliation, Non-aggression and Exchanges and Cooperation, and the Provisions on Non-aggression agreed in September 1992. These agreements are based on principles of 'transparency' and 'constraint', often mutually reinforcing. Transparency involves steps that make hostile intentions difficult to conceal. These include:

- notification measures (such as publishing the nature and scale of planned military exercises);
- communication measures (such as maintaining hot-lines and other instruments for crisis management);
- information measures (including providing defence budget data and information on force composition);
- and procedures for observation and verification of military exercises and manoeuvres.

Constraint involves agreements designed to limit a country's ability to launch a surprise attack or reduce the potential for damage in the event of such an attack. Constraint measures include:

- limitations on the production and deployment of specific weapons systems;
- and restrictions on the size and type of forces deployed in a particular theatre.[6]

To date, North and South Korea have had great difficulty implementing these types of measures due to residual suspicions and periodic flare-ups between the two states. To overcome these serious barriers to trust-building, the two sides could start with modest and non-intrusive initiatives. They might begin, for example, with exchanges of military information and discussions about doctrine and strategy. As confidence about the other side's intentions increases over time, more concrete measures could be attempted. These might include the relocation of North Korea's long-range artillery systems away from the demilitarised zone, the conversion of the DMZ into a peace zone and the suspension, for a specified period of time, of the annual US–South Korean *Team Spirit* exercises.

If some or all of the above trust-building initiatives can be implemented, and barring a new crisis on the peninsula, a specific plan could be drawn up for the gradual reduction of US Forces, Korea (USFK), personnel. This type of commitment should not be made, however, until adequate safeguards are in place to ensure that Pyongyang cannot renege on specific commitments once US forces have been removed. This might require UN monitoring teams to have extensive access to North Korean bases and weapons-production centres. Tunnels and other venues for concealment would need to be made accessible for reliable monitoring. Pyongyang would also have to end its boycott of the UN Command's Military Armistice Commission meetings and reverse its decision to seal off the DMZ territory under its control. No real trust-building can take place until the issues of access and jurisdiction raised by these North Korean actions are resolved.

The US should also act to minimise politico-economic tensions with South Korea that could be exploited by the North. Ongoing trade differences, for example, should be negotiated quietly and with flexibility from the US side, at least until the prospects for Korean re-unification are more advanced. Above all, the US Congress should resist linking South Korean trade practices with US security commitments to the ROK.

A more cautious approach would reduce the risk of increased anti-US sentiment among farmers, labour organisations and small business groups and other components of the South Korean middle class. It would also ensure that South Korea – and, eventually, a unified Korea – remains committed to the free-trade principles of APEC's Bogor Declaration without having to face incessant US pressure to restructure domestic marketing practices.

Korea and the Regional Balance
How should US strategy adjust should a unified Korea emerge into the Asia-Pacific power balance? US defence planners need to begin to think about ways to shift US policy away from the Cold War reliance on a large ground presence in South Korea towards a more mobile force capable of working with other North-east Asian states to achieve common strategic goals. If Korean unification succeeds, the US force structure on the peninsula could be reduced and

reconfigured. The US Army's Second Infantry Division (with currently just over 27,000 personnel) could be gradually reduced, and remaining US ground forces could become part of what General Colin Powell has termed 'adaptive joint force packages'. These would combine US and allied units that could operate jointly and conduct combined force operations in a regional security environment more susceptible to local conflicts than to great-power confrontation.[7] All this is consistent with the Base Force strategy's emphasis on projecting future US military power from continental US locations.

It also accords with the South Korean government's long-term goals, as articulated by its Minister of National Defence, Lee Yang-Ho. He has speculated on the transition from 'the ROK–US defence alliance, which makes preparations for a North Korean threat, to a future-oriented security partnership which contributes to regional security and peace'. Lee has also discussed the potential for 'military exchange programmes and co-operation with neighbouring countries'.[8] The United States could contribute to this long-term goal by helping to train members of the South Korean military to work more directly and effectively with members of the Japanese SDF, both to bolster Seoul's sense of security and to reassure Tokyo about the future stability of the peninsula. Although historical and political tensions still encumber Japanese–South Korean relations, it is undoubtedly in the interests of both countries to develop closer military ties. Both Tokyo and Seoul are beginning to recognise the benefits of selective collaboration on issues of security and defence, and US policy-makers should do what they can to encourage this trend. For example, the US might support specific forms of Japanese–South Korean military collaboration, including mine-clearing and anti-submarine warfare activities designed to prepare for threats to commercial shipping routes in the Sea of Japan. The use of local anti-submarine assets to clear these routes would release US nuclear submarines for missions more directly related to deterrence and escalation control against a regional aggressor.

China–Taiwan
As demonstrated by the repercussions from Lee Teng-hui's visit to the United States, the fundamental challenge for US security policy in the Taiwan Strait is to strike an effective balance between honouring the US commitment to a 'one China' policy and supporting Taiwan's continued development of an independent economic and political identity without fear of Chinese military intimidation. On

the one hand, for the United States to challenge this basic premise of Chinese sovereignty – which it accepted at the time it normalised relations with China – would entail unacceptable risks to regional stability. On the other hand, reducing its support for a democratically elected Taiwanese government would enrage powerful members of the US Congress, and impede the cause of peaceful democratic change in other Asia-Pacific locales. The US should therefore engage China regularly on the issue of Taiwan through various diplomatic channels, expressing its concern that Taipei remain a prosperous and positive force for regional economic and political development.

Striking a judicious balance with China and Taiwan in its political relations does not prevent the US from undertaking independent measures to reinforce the credibility of the Taiwan Relations Act at appropriate intervals. The United States should retain its prerogative to transfer large quantities of modern weapons to Taiwan in the event of a future crisis with China – in direct proportion to the threat involved. Upgrading of command, control, communications and intelligence (C3I) systems and the deployment of more advanced defensive missile systems and anti-submarine warfare capabilities would be appropriate measures if Taiwan were threatened with an imminent Chinese attack. If China takes military action to intimidate Taiwan, the US could also introduce AWACS into the East China Sea to track Chinese military deployments opposite Taiwan and signal its resolution to honour the TRA.

The Clinton administration and its successors can help reassure Taiwan and deter China by publicly reiterating the principles articulated by the Reagan administration in 1982:

- not to agree to set a date for ending arms sales to Taiwan;
- not to consult Beijing prior to such arms sales;
- not to mediate between Taipei and Beijing;
- not to revise the Taiwan Relations Act;
- not to abandon its commitment to oppose any Chinese use of force to resolve the Taiwan issue;
- and not to pressure Taiwan to enter into negotiations with the PRC.

The United States might also bolster its deterrent message to Beijing by asserting that China would pay a heavy economic and diplomatic price for any acts of aggression against Taiwan. To drive this point home, the US could assert publicly that it would cancel China's most favoured nation status if it launches an attack across the Taiwan Strait. This type of statement is more realistic and, therefore, likely to be more effective than any new military warnings. It might also pre-empt more controversial and riskier initiatives by members of the US Congress.

US policy-makers should continue to assure the Taiwanese that they will not be abandoned in the event of an unprovoked Chinese invasion. At the same time, the United States needs to make it clear to Taiwan that it will continue to support the goal of cross-Strait re-unification. Minor adjustments in US policy regarding official contacts with the Taiwanese government may be necessary and even useful in the future.[9] But public speculation by members of either the executive or the legislative branches of the US government about US support for Taiwanese sovereignty will inevitably incite emotional and hostile responses from Beijing and needlessly increase the risk of a US–China conflict.

The South China Sea
For reasons discussed in Chapter 3, it is highly unlikely that the US will permit itself to be pulled into any future military confrontation in the South China Sea that does not directly threaten US national-security interests. It is also highly unlikely that regional states will be motivated by this consideration to create a reliable multilateral defence organisation of their own. In these circumstances, US policy-makers need to pursue a fall-back strategy of assisting ASEAN member-states in their efforts at conflict resolution and crisis prevention in the South China Sea. In the short term at least, the United States can make its greatest contribution to such a campaign by maintaining sufficient naval forces in the region to back up its commitment to protect international maritime traffic.

Whether or not the US military is adequately prepared to accomplish this task is a matter of considerable debate and concern. This explains Commander-in-Chief of the US Pacific Command Admiral Richard Macke's early 1995 recommendation to establish a Readiness Preservation Authority to provide 'timely supplemental funds for unplanned contingencies' and to stop the current US government practice of shifting funds out of current readiness accounts designated for the Pacific Command (PACOM) and other commands.[10] This is a sensible proposal, but it will need to be integrated into a more comprehensive strategy for ensuring the security of Asia-Pacific waterways. Such a strategy will have to rely more on regional friends and allies for the provision of military personnel, firepower and logistical support in the initial stages of any future regional conflict.

The US Navy's current doctrinal thinking assumes that such regional support will be forthcoming. The Navy's September 1992 White Paper, ...*From the Sea: Preparing the Naval Service for the 21st Century*, places primary emphasis on the development of naval and air assets that are necessary for combined-arms operations close to shores.[11] It presumes that offshore friends and allies will provide greater support to sustain such operations as mine-sweeping, straits control and coastal defence against amphibious assaults. The document's premise is questionable, however, due to its failure to explain how US and allied fleet assets can be integrated to fulfil the missions it envisions. ...*From the Sea* is also too optimistic in its assumption that the US will continue to enjoy unchallenged command of the open oceans, at a time when the Clinton administration plans to reduce overall US naval strength by 55 surface ships and submarines, one aircraft carrier, and one active and one reserve naval air wing.[12]

The United States needs to find new ways to compensate for its gradual naval disengagement from the Asia-Pacific. One way to accomplish this, without placing an undue burden on the US defence budget, is to expand Rim of the Pacific (RIMPAC) exercises to involve more regional friends and allies and encourage new patterns of naval cooperation between countries like Japan and South Korea. The United States could also pursue arrangements for *ad hoc* defence cooperation with key regional actors based on the models of the Memoranda of Understanding that the US has already negotiated with Indonesia, Malaysia and Singapore for limited logistical support.

Closer US cooperation with members of the Five Power Defence Arrangements (FPDA) could also be investigated. The principal rationale for increased US defence cooperation with the FPDA countries (Australia, Malaysia, Singapore, New Zealand and the UK) is a common interest in effective surveillance and patrol activities in and around the Strait of Malacca. US Assistant Secretary of Defense for International Security Joseph Nye recently asserted that US naval vessels 'would be prepared to escort and make sure that free navigation continues' in the event of a military conflict that threatens navigation in the South China Sea.[13] FPDA members should be pressed to assist in any such operation.

The September 1994 FPDA manoeuvres in the South China Sea illustrate that such multilateral security cooperation is possible, and that it can be done in a low-key and non-provocative manner. FPDA defence ministers emphasised that the exercise site was not selected to put pressure on China, but rather to expand FPDA coverage to

Sarawak and Sabah off Malaysia's eastern coast, and to the state of Brunei, in case the Sultanate accepted the invitation to join the Five Power group.[14] The fact that Beijing may not have believed these assurances does not undermine the usefulness of such statements.

Pursuing new modes of defence cooperation while concurrently reassuring Asian states of its benign intentions is likely to become a common US practice over the next decade. US policy-makers and the American public have always been uncomfortable with this type of diplomacy. It is nonetheless an indispensable lubricant for moderate multipolar balancing in the region and, as such, it is a skill that the US will have to master.

Encouraging ASEAN Self-Reliance
As it adjusts to a new role in Asia, the United States will need to take care not to pre-empt the ASEAN member-states as they move cautiously and incrementally towards multilateral security cooperation. At a minimum, US policy-makers will need to be more 'region-centric' in their statements regarding South-east Asia, in order to counterbalance the effects of the Navy's 'places not bases' campaign, which many in the region perceive as a globalist approach and more oriented towards the protection of US and European oil supplies in the Middle East. At the same time, US policy-makers should continue to assert America's right to intervene unilaterally in the event that its vital interests are compromised or international maritime traffic is threatened. Taken together, these policies would align US interests with those of its regional friends and allies without jeopardising the prospects for intra-ASEAN cooperation. A continued US offshore military presence in South-east Asia is a precondition for the success of such a campaign.

One measure of the success of a new US strategy of reassurance in South-east Asia will be the continued growth of informal networks of security planners within the ARF or other regional fora. But the ultimate success of such a campaign will be illustrated by the extent to which indigenous defence-related institutions are transformed from 'talking shops' into effective elements of a regional balance-of-power system. Over the last decade, ASEAN member-states have pursued substantial conventional force modernisation programmes while engaging in negotiations to establish region-wide mechanisms for mutual reassurance and conflict avoidance. At present, the 'China threat' provides the greatest impetus for ASEAN states to move towards more substantive defence cooperation. In future, however, the most immediate threats to South-east Asian states may come from within ASEAN itself, which has no shortage of unre-solved disputes between its members. Indonesia and Malaysia both claim the Sipadan and Ligitan islands near Indonesia's Kalimantan province; Brunei and Malaysia are at odds over the Sultanate's claim to an EEZ in an area of the South China Sea that Kuala Lumpur considers part of its territory; and residual ethnic tensions in the Malay archipelago complex are still a source of intra-regional tensions. As far as possible, the US should assist ASEAN states in developing conflict-resolution and preventive-diplomacy pro-grammes before these issues become intractable. Australia's Minis-ter for Foreign Affairs, Gareth Evans, has proposed a number of measures that might benefit from US participation or support. These include:

- expanding existing 'incidents at sea' agreements (currently in-volving the US, UK and Russia) to include other Asia-Pacific actors;
- establishing a maritime surveillance and safety regime in the region;
- enhancing transparency through the exchange of selected intelli-gence data and monitoring of various military exercises.[15]

As it attempts to contribute to the evolving intra-ASEAN security dialogue, the US will discover that it still has some leverage among South-east Asian states because of the interest that virtually all members of ASEAN have in keeping a US naval presence in the region. At the same time, ASEAN states feel secure and confident enough to demand a different kind of relationship with the United States. ASEAN's criticism of President Clinton's policy of enlarge-ment was a reflection of this new assertiveness. A joint memorandum released in December 1993 by the ASEAN Institutes of Strategic and International Studies questioned the extent to which the United States could play a meaningful role in regional security affairs in the future due to its bilateral 'diplomatic difficulties with some countries in the region over issues such as trade imbalance ... democracy, human rights and its perceived reduced political will over crises in Somalia and Bosnia'.[16]

Free Trade
The future of Asia-Pacific security will be determined in large part by the degree of economic cooperation among Asian states. And US influence over the evolving Asia-Pacific security dialogue will de-pend upon its ability to improve US access to regional markets. The

US can bolster regional economic cooperation while protecting US economic interests by pursuing three strategies:

- US policy-makers can continue to press – firmly but diplomatically – for the removal of structural barriers that currently threaten both US–Japan economic relations and the US–Japan alliance.
- The United States can assist China in becoming more involved in the institutions and processes of the liberal world economy.
- US officials can encourage the growing sense of community in the Asia-Pacific, while opposing efforts by various Asian governments to create an exclusive trading bloc at US expense.

Reconciling With Japan

The first step to improving the US bilateral relationship with Japan is for Washington to reaffirm publicly that US–Japan defence cooperation is still the highest priority in the bilateral relationship. In the midst of loud and acrimonious trade disputes, and against a backdrop of the fiftieth anniversary of the end of the Pacific War and the bombing of Hiroshima and Nagasaki, this still-obvious point can be easily missed. Indeed, there is no shortage of commentators in both Japan and the United States who have asserted that in a post-Cold War international system 'geo-economics' has replaced geopolitics as the top priority for all states. But as Nye has recently observed, 'international economic systems rest upon international political order', and there can be no reliable political order in the Asia-Pacific without US–Japan defence cooperation.[17] Critical issues that demand joint action by the US and Japan include the challenge of Chinese power; the perpetual tension on the Korean peninsula and, in the future, the regional implications of North–South Korean reunification; the repercussions in North-east Asia from the collapse of the Soviet Union; and the need for security cooperation between North-east and South-east Asian states.

Tokyo will continue to have difficulty working with the US to manage these regional challenges until it becomes a more 'normal' member of the Asia-Pacific community of states. Even with active US support, there are strict limits on what Japan can do diplomatically and, in particular, militarily in Asia. Much of its activity will only be possible under a United Nations banner. Even then, it is worth noting that Japan's modest peacekeeping initiatives in Cambodia and Africa elicited intense criticism both inside and outside Japan. Persistent cultural and historical barriers make it both risky and difficult for Tokyo to go much further with such initiatives, or to take a leading role in regional debates about multilateral security cooperation. Furthermore, for the foreseeable future Japanese governments are likely to be composed of fragile coalitions which will have extraordinary difficulty in pursuing long-term foreign-policy goals. The domestic problems that the Murayama goverment is facing in late 1995 as a result of the Okinawa rape case is a dramatic illustration of this.

These are just some of the reasons why the US–Japan Mutual Security Treaty is still the one clear imperative in Japanese security policy. But the MST has begun to suffer collateral damage from persistent and intense US–Japanese trade disputes. The US needs to continue to pressure Japan to lower its import barriers (in particular, its non-tariff barriers), but it should assure its most important Asian ally that it will no longer resort to unilateral actions, like short-term numerical quotas, to move the process forward.

For three reasons in particular, future US–Japan trade disputes should be brought to the WTO for resolution. First, the multilateral nature of the WTO will help both governments to manage better their respective nationalistic constituencies. 'Japan-bashing' has been a popular sport among US politicians and pundits for some time, but in recent years there has been a reciprocal growth in anti-Americanism on the Japanese side. Both sides have a strong interest in reigning in these tendencies. A second reason for according priority to the WTO has to do with its exclusively economic mandate. Relying on the WTO for the resolution of trade disputes will make it easier for both Tokyo and Washington to prevent trade issues from spilling over into the realm of joint-security cooperation. Finally, the Clinton administration has an interest in enhancing the prestige and influence of the WTO because President Clinton's sponsorship of the organisation was one of his most important foreign-policy successes. It would be a tragic error and a major setback for global free trade if the United States were to undermine the WTO by triggering a trade war.

While it negotiates with Japan within the WTO framework, the United States would be well advised to develop policies that encourage Japan to take greater responsibility for the future global economic order. For example, US officials could press Japan to increase its contribution to the International Monetary Fund (IMF) and the World Bank. At present, Tokyo provides 7.43% of World Bank funds and 5.85% of IMF funds, compared to US contributions of 17.9% and 18.17%, respectively. A more equitable arrangement would be to increase the Japanese contribution to both institutions to two-thirds the amount provided by the US. In return, Washington could undertake to accord Tokyo greater influence over the decisions taken within both organisations.

This policy change could be part of a larger US effort to help Japan raise its profile within the United Nations system. Thus, while the US presses Japan to increase its contribution to the IMF and the World Bank, it could intensify its support for Japanese efforts to obtain a permanent seat on the UN Security Council. The US delegation to the UN could also press for the deletion of the 'former enemy states' clauses (articles 53 and 107) from the United Nations Charter.

The US could also cooperate more closely with Japan in the formulation of policies regarding international lending and foreign aid. To date, US policy-makers have not accorded Tokyo the status it deserves as the world's largest source of overseas development assistance (supplying over $12bn annually), while Japanese decisions with regard to international lending and foreign aid have often been based on narrow and self-serving considerations. By coordinating lending and aid activities, the US and Japan can still advance their national interests, but are likely to have a more positive impact where they recognise a common regional or global interest.

US policy-makers should also intensify their support for Japanese efforts to reconcile with key Asia-Pacific states. As a first step, the US could cooperate with Japan to help insure the South Korean government against financial collapse if it were presented with a 'German problem' following a sudden collapse of the North Korean regime. Quiet discussions on such issues as currency stabilisation and capital infusion might help to avert a major crisis on the peninsula in the future. Such discussions would also go a long way towards improving the still-tense relationship between Seoul and Tokyo to the benefit of overall regional security.

The US could also actively support Japan's attempt to raise its profile within APEC. The November 1995 APEC summit in Osaka was to have been an important step forward in Japan's efforts to establish a leading role for itself within this regional organisation. The results of the summit were disappointing in all respects, however, due in large part to President Clinton's last-minute decision not to attend in view of unavoidable domestic political problems. The United States, therefore, must now redouble its efforts to support a new Japanese role in Asia.

Future US cooperation with Japan will inevitably depend upon Tokyo's continued willingness to support, rather than exploit, the

US–Japan defence relationship. Japan should weigh very carefully the issue of funding for US forces in Japan, in light of the US public's sensitivity to the issue of defence burden-sharing. It is both politically unwise and logically indefensible for Japanese politicians to question their government's host-nation support programmes on the grounds that a substantial portion of the US military forces stationed in Japan have designated responsibilities that extend beyond Japanese territory, since virtually all of these missions help to establish the essential context for Japan's security. Tokyo needs to make this argument forcefully and repeatedly to its public as part of a larger campaign of public information in support of the Mutual Security Treaty. A comparable campaign of public information is also required on the US side.

Assimilating China

China's trading partners within APEC need to become more adept at both encouraging and exploiting the PRC's integration into the global and regional economies. In particular, China's growing dependence on external sources of financing and high-technology goods can provide Asia-Pacific states with considerable leverage in their relations with Beijing. Some experts have also predicted that China will become increasingly dependent upon external sources for its agricultural and energy needs in the near future. The US can and should take the lead in a campaign to use the leverage that these new trade links can provide by pursuing a long-term strategy of 'positive conditionality' towards China.[18] For example, the US should continue to insist that China comply with WTO rules of entry and behaviour if it wishes to become a WTO member. Such rules affect Chinese decisions about intellectual property rights, labour standards and foreign direct investment.

Pursuing Free Trade Throughout the Asia-Pacific

The single most important economic policy that the United States can undertake in the next few years is to intensify its support for the full integration of the Asia-Pacific region into the global system of free trade. This will not be easy for the United States since an institutionalised, rule-based system of free trade will sometimes be seen as an economic problem by a US government that is no longer capable of dominating the world economy. Because the industrialising and post-industrial economies of East Asia are among the world's fastest growing economies, yet are also its worst exploiters of the liberal free trade regime, it is imperative that the US pursue a regional strategy designed to preserve the stability of this high growth area while simultaneously expanding US access to its markets.

The United States will have to continue to bargain hard with its Asia-Pacific trading partners over the next decade. Whenever possible, however, the US should resist the temptation to engage in unilateral arm-twisting and instead take its case to multilateral institutions like APEC and the WTO. APEC is especially attractive as a forum for regional cooperation, since it provides a context for such diverse countries as China, Japan and the United States to discuss and identify their common economic interests.

Given its stake in APEC's progress, recent efforts by the United States to increase its agricultural exports at the expense of some APEC members are particularly ill-advised. Scrapping the Export Enhancement Program (EEP), which subsidises US farmers, would set an example for states like Japan and some European Union states by demonstrating that the US is prepared to override domestic interest-group pressures to achieve the common goal of rule-based free trade.

The agricultural issue illustrates the problems that the Clinton administration and its successors will continue to face in their efforts to enhance US access to growing Asian markets while protecting US jobs and wages. It is important for US policy-makers to keep in mind that these two goals are not mutually exclusive; America's long-term interests are best served by the pursuit of intra-APEC investment opportunities that gradually increase US access to Asian markets.

Conclusion

The policy recommendations presented in this chapter do not constitute a grand strategy for the United States in the Asia-Pacific. Rather, they are proposals for a number of steps designed to help establish a moderate multipolar balance-of-power system in the Asia-Pacific over the next decade. In such a system, the day-to-day interactions of regional states would be constrained not only by the cautionary dynamics of power balancing, but also by conventions of diplomatic consultation and expectations of mutual economic benefit.

Multipolarity will place much greater demands on US diplomacy than the Cold War did. US interests in the Asia-Pacific will be harder to define and harder to defend unilaterally. US leaders will also have greater difficulty explaining these interests, and justifying actions in support of them, to influential domestic constituencies. To succeed, US policy-makers will need to accord a higher priority to Asia *per se*, as opposed to the Cold War practice of treating the Asia-Pacific as an adjunct to the US global campaign of anti-communist containment. If US policy-makers are unable to make fundamental changes in the way they formulate, execute and explain US foreign policy in the Asia-Pacific, the relevance of the United States as an actor in this region is likely to dwindle in the early twenty-first century.

Notes

Chapter I

1 James A. Baker, III, 'America in Asia: Emerging Architecture for a Pacific Community', *Foreign Affairs*, vol. 70, no. 5, Winter 1991–92, p. 4.

2 *Report of the Secretary of Defense to the President and the Congress* (Washington, DC: US Government Printing Office (USGPO), 1993), p. 3.

3 Patrick E. Tyler, 'US Strategy Plan Calls for Ensuring No Rivals Develop', *New York Times*, 8 March 1992, p. 1; and 'Excerpts from the Pentagon's Plan: "Prevent the Re-emergence of a New Rival"', *ibid.*, A14.

4 For a critique of the preponderance strategy reflecting concerns raised in Congress and elsewhere, see Christopher Layne, 'The Unipolar Illusion: Why Great Powers Will Rise', *International Security*, vol. 17, no. 4, Spring 1993, pp. 8–16.

5 Paul D. Wolfowitz, 'The New Defense Strategy', in Graham Allison and Gregory F. Treverton (eds), *Rethinking America's Security* (New York: W.W. Norton, 1992), pp. 176–95.

6 '1992 Joint Military Net Assessment', Joint Staff, Directorate for Force Structure, Resources, and Assessment, J-8, Washington DC, August 1992, pp. 2.3–2.5 and 7.1–10.18.

7 US Department of Defense, *A Strategic Framework for the Asia-Pacific Rim: A Report to Congress* (Washington DC: USGPO, 1992), pp. 2–5; and US Department of Defense, *A Strategic Framework for the Asian Pacific Rim: Looking Toward the 21st Century* (Washington DC: USGPO, 1990).

8 *Report of the Secretary of Defense*, p. 12.

9 '1992 Joint Military Net Assessment', pp. 3–7.

10 *A Strategic Framework [1992]*, p. 2.

11 Alan Tonelson, 'Superpower Without a Sword', *Foreign Affairs*, vol. 72, no. 3, Summer 1993, pp. 173–74.

12 Dov Z. Zackheim and Jeffrey M. Ranney, 'Matching Defense Strategies and Resources: Challenges for the Clinton Administration', *International Security*, vol. 18, no. 1, Summer 1993, p. 71.

13 'Bush, Clinton Offer Views of Policies Toward Asia', *Asian Wall Street Journal Weekly*, 26 October 1992, p. 1. See also, 'Economy, Defense, Democracy to be the US Policy Pillars', United States Information Service (USIS), *Wireless File*, 13 January 1993.

14 'Lord: Elements of Democracy Necessary for Modernization', USIS, *Wireless File*, 31 March 1993.

15 'Who Needs a Vision?', *The Bulletin* (Sydney), 5 April 1993, p. 53.

16 For excerpts from Lake's address to the Council on Foreign Relations, see 'Effective Engagement in a Changing World', USIS, *Wireless File*, 17 December 1993.

17 See Shalikashvili's address to the National Defense University, Washington DC, 'US Military Strategy for the 1990s', USIS, *Wireless File*, 17 March 1994.

18 See Larson's Congressional testimony in 'Cooperative Engagement and Economic Security in Asia', USIS, *Wireless File*, 10 March 1993, p. 53.

19 James Winnefeld, *et al.*, *A New Strategy and Fewer Forces: the*

Pacific Dimension, R-4089/2-USDP
(Santa Monica, CA: RAND, 1992).
[20] The first version of the *Bottom-Up
Review* appeared in September; the
full version appeared in October.
See US Secretary of Defense Les
Aspin, *The Bottom-Up Review:
Forces For a New Era* (Washington
DC: US Department of Defense,
1993), p. 11; and Aspin, 'Supple-
mentary Report of the Bottom-Up
Review', October 1993, p. 20.
[21] Robert L. Borosage, 'Inventing
the Threat: Clinton's Defence
Budget', *World Policy Journal*, vol.
10, no. 4, Winter 1993–94, p. 7. See
also Dennis S. Ippolito, *Blunting the
Sword: Budget Policy and the
Future of Defense* (Washington DC:
NDU Press, 1994), pp. 39–104.
[22] Seth Cropsey, 'Bottom Line
Versus Front Line', *Defender*
(Canberra), vol. 11, no. 1, Autumn
1993, pp. 27–29; and Eliot Cohen,
'Beyond Bottom-Up', *National
Review*, 15 November 1993, pp. 40–
43.
[23] Aspin, 'Report of the Bottom-up
Review', p. 16.
[24] Center for Defense Information,
'America's Military Role in the
New World Order: Have Guns Will
Travel', *The Defense Monitor*, vol.
22, no. 7, 1993, p. 6.
[25] Remarks by Winston Lord before
the Overseas Press Club and the
Asia Society, 18 January 1994, in
USIS, *Official Text*, 2 February
1994.
[26] Editorial in *Korea Times*, 13 July
1993, p. 6, in *Foreign Broadcast
Information Service* (*FBIS*) EAS, 13
July 1993, p. 26.
[27] US Department of Defense, Office
of International Security Affairs,
*United States Security Strategy for
the East-Asia-Pacific Region*
(Washington DC: USGPO, 1995).

[28] Jonathan Pollack, *Designing a
New American Security Strategy for
Asia* (New York: Council on
Foreign Relations, 1995), p. 32.
[29] *United States Security Strategy*, p.
11.
[30] In a subsequent article in *Foreign
Affairs*, US Assistant Secretary of
Defense for International Security,
Joseph S. Nye Jr, went further in
attempting to close the conceptual
gap between the administration's
commitment to bilateral arrangements and its interest in
multilateralism. While potentially
useful, his arguments are nonetheless very general. See 'The Case For
Deep Engagement', *Foreign Affairs*,
vol. 74, no. 2, July/August 1995, pp.
101–102.
[31] Yoichi Funibashi, 'The
Asianization of Asia', *Foreign
Affairs*, vol. 72, no. 5, November/
December 1993, pp. 75–85.
[32] Robert Scalapino, 'The United
States and Asia: Future Prospects',
Foreign Affairs, vol. 70, no. 5,
Winter 1991–92, p. 38.
[33] See Robert Garran, 'Japan's
Security Dilemma', *The Weekend
Australian*, 28–29 October 1995, p.
30; and Nicholas Kristof, 'Tokyo
Fails to Resolve Bases Impasse',
New York Times, 5 November 1995,
p. 13.

Chapter II
[1] Gerald Segal, 'What Can We Do
About Nuclear Forces in Northeast
Asia?', *The Korean Journal of
Defense Analysis*, vol. 6, no. 2,
Winter 1994, pp. 37–38.
[2] Dunbar Lockwood, 'The Status of
US, Russian and Chinese Nuclear
Forces in Northeast Asia', *Arms
Control Today*, November 1994, pp.
23–24.
[3] Kishore Mahbubani, 'The Pacific

Impulse', *Survival*, vol. 37, no. 1, Spring 1995, p. 107. Data is from William Rees-Mogg, 'Money Moves East, as Welfare Goes West', *Straits Times* (Singapore), 9 July 1994, p. 35.

[4] Gerald Segal, *China Changes Shape: Regionalism and Foreign Policy*, Adelphi Paper 287 (London: Brassey's for the IISS, 1994), p. 3.

[5] See Nicholas Lardy, *China in the World Economy* (Washington DC: Institute for International Economics, 1994), especially pp. 105–16. Regarding China's growing agricultural needs, see Joseph Kahn, 'As Industry Devours Land, China's Grain Imports Soar', *Asian Wall Street Journal*, 13 March 1995, pp. 1 and 7.

[6] For a general assessment, see the Directorate of Intelligence, Central Intelligence Agency, *China's Economy in 1993 and 1994: The Search for a Soft Landing*, EA 94-10016 (Washington DC: USGPO, 1994), pp. 20–21.

[7] James Fallows, *Looking At the Sun* (New York: Pantheon Books, 1994), p. 247.

[8] Todd S. Purdum, 'Bradley Rebukes Clinton on Japan', *New York Times*, 24 February 1994, p. D1.

[9] The phrase is borrowed from Joshua Muravchik's well-known book, *Exporting Democracy: Fulfilling America's Destiny* (Washington DC: AEI Press, 1991).

[10] Muthiah Alagappa offers an excellent summary of the basic premises of enlargement, in *Democratic Transition in Asia: The Role of the International Community*, East-West Center Special Reports No. 3 (Honolulu, HI: East-West Center, 1994), pp. 4–6. See also the statement by US National Security Adviser Anthony Lake, 'From Containment to Engagement', *Vital Speeches of the Day*, vol. 60, no. 1, 15 October 1993, pp. 15–16; and Assistant Secretary of State for Democracy, Human Rights, and Labor, John Shattuck, 'Vienna and Beyond: US Human Rights Diplomacy in the Post-Cold War World', Keynote Address to the Union Internationale des Avocats, San Francisco, CA, 29 August 1993.

[11] Robert A. Manning and Paula Stern, 'The Myth of the Pacific Community', *Foreign Affairs*, vol. 73, no. 6, November/December 1994, pp. 86–87.

[12] *Ibid.*, p. 87.

[13] Kishore Mahbubani, 'The Dangers of Decadence', *Foreign Affairs*, vol. 72, no. 4, September/October 1993, p. 13. See also the commentary by Frank Ching on the recent US report to the UN Human Rights Commission in 'US Role On Rights Reversed', *Far Eastern Economic Review*, 22 June 1995, p. 40.

Chapter III

[1] Testimony of General Robert Riscassi, Commander-in-Chief of the US–ROK Combined Forces Command before the US Senate Armed Forces Committee, 21 April 1993, USIS, *Wireless File*, 21 April 1993; 'Attack Across the DMZ', *Jane's Intelligence Review*, Special Report No. 2, vol. 6, no. 4, April 1993, pp. 22–24.

[2] Paul Bracken, 'Risks and Promises in the Two Koreas', *Orbis,* vol. 39, no. 1, Winter 1995, p. 57; and Bracken, 'Nuclear Weapons and State Survival in North Korea', *Survival*, vol. 35, no. 3, Autumn 1993, p. 141.

[3] The full text of the Agreed Framework can be found in BBC, *Summary of World Broadcasts* FE/2134/

D/1–2, 24 October 1994.

[4] Ambassador Robert L. Gallucci, the primary US negotiator, provides one of the most comprehensive US accounts of this argument. See his testimony before the US Senate Foreign Relations Subcommittee on East Asian and Pacific Affairs, USIS, *Wireless File*, 1 December 1994.

[5] Larry A. Niksch, 'Opportunities and Challenges in Clinton's Confidence-Building Strategy Towards North Korea', *The Korean Journal of Defense Analysis,* vol. 6, no. 2, Winter 1994, p. 151.

[6] Ted Galen Carpenter, 'Ending South Korea's Unhealthy Security Dependence', *The Korean Journal of Defense Analysis*, vol. 4, no. 1, Summer 1994, pp. 188–89. See also, Doug Bandow, 'Unfreezing Korea', *The National Interest*, no. 25, Autumn 1991, pp. 51–58.

[7] Ronald Steel, *Temptations of a Superpower* (Cambridge, MA: Harvard University Press, 1995), pp. 102–20 and 128.

[8] Institute for National Strategic Studies, *Strategic Assessment 1995* (Washington DC: USGPO, 1995), p. 25.

[9] Thomas Schelling, *The Strategy of Conflict* (Cambridge, MA: Harvard University Press, 1960), p. 232.

[10] Mark Clifford, 'The Pressures of Winning', *Far Eastern Economic Review*, vol. 158, no. 25, 22 June 1995, pp. 42–44.

[11] In November 1995 ('a banner year for ill-timed remarks by Japanese lawmakers about Korea'), Japanese Minister Takami Eto was forced to resign after remarking that Japan did 'some good things' for Korea before and during the Second World War. See Hijiri Inose, *Nikkei Weekly*, 13 November 1995, p. 4.

[12] See the 'Full Text of President Kim's Statement at New Year's Press Conference', *Korea Observer*, vol. 36, no. 1, Spring 1995, pp. 117–23.

[13] See Harry Harding's discussion of an internal memo reportedly authored in spring 1994 by Winston Lord, 'Asia Policy to the Brink', *Foreign Policy*, no. 96, Autumn 1994, p. 71.

[14] Gary Klintworth, 'Taiwan', in J. Mohan Malik, *Asian Defence Policies: Regional Conflicts and Security Issues* (Geelong, Victoria: Deakin University Press, 1994), p. 71.

[15] For an expanded analysis of these perspectives, see Ronald Montaperto and Ming Zhang, 'The Taiwan Issue: A Test of Sino–US Relations', *The Journal of Contemporary China*, no. 9, Summer 1995, pp. 8–11.

[16] For excerpts and analysis, see Mark S. Pratt, 'US Reactions to the PRC Use of Force Against Taiwan', in Parris H. Chang and Martin L. Lasater (eds), *If China Crosses the Taiwan Strait: The International Response* (New York: Lanham, 1993), p. 41.

[17] Li Jiaquan, 'Lee's US Visit Defies Agreement', *Beijing Review*, vol. 38, no. 26, 26 June–2 July 1995, p. 19. Li is Director of the Institute of Taiwan Studies of the Chinese Academy of Social Sciences in Beijing.

[18] Julian Baum, 'A Case of Nerves', *Far Eastern Economic Review*, vol. 158, no. 29, 20 July 1995, p. 26.

[19] See Peter Wilson, 'Gingrich Plays China Policy by the Book', *The Weekend Australian*, 22–23 July 1995, p. 14.

[20] The Taiwanese are highly sensitive to the *Kilo* purchases and have

tracked their movements from shipyards in northern Europe to Chinese ports in the Pacific. See 'The First of the Four Russian-Built Submarines Purchased by Mainland China Passes Through the Strait of Malacca', *Lien Ho Pao* (Hong Kong), 20 February 1995, p. 2, in *FBIS*-CHI, 21 February 1995, p. 1.

[21] Michael Swaine, 'Arms Races and Threats Across the Taiwan Straits', paper delivered at a conference, 'Chinese Economic Reform: The Impact on Security Policy', sponsored by the International Institute for Strategic Studies and the Chinese Council of Advanced Policy Studies (Taiwan), Hong Kong, 8–10 July 1994, pp. 10–11.

[22] Michael Swaine, private communication, October 1995; and Godwin, 'Use of Military Force', pp. 25–26.

[23] Godwin, 'Use of Military Force', p. 26; Swaine, 'Arms Races and Threats', p. 17; Gary Klintworth, 'Developments in Taiwan's Maritime Security', *Issues and Studies*, vol. 30, no. 1, January 1994, p. 73; and, for foreign analysts cited, see Nayan Chanda, *et al.*, 'Fear of the Dragon', *Far Eastern Economic Review*, vol. 158, no. 15, 13 April 1995, p. 26.

[24] Ross Munro, 'Eavesdropping on the Chinese Military: Where It Expects War – Where It Doesn't', *Orbis*, vol. 38, no. 3, Summer 1994, p. 358.

[25] Julian Baum, 'Idling Threat', *Far Eastern Economic Review*, vol. 158, no. 15, 13 April 1994, p. 29.

[26] A Hong Kong daily, *Cheng Ming* (Contending), reported in February 1995 that key Chinese defence officials held a meeting in late December 1994 to consider the Taiwan issue and recommended that the matter of reunification be resolved soon due to Taiwanese President Li Teng-hui's collaboration with Western authorities in an anti-China strategy. See Yi Fan, 'Chinese Communists Prepare Public Opinion for Attacking Taiwan with Force', *Cheng Ming*, 1 February 1995, pp. 25–26, in *FBIS*-CHI, 14 April 1995, pp. 22–24.

[27] See Michael Y. M. Kau, 'US Visit Fits the Realities of Taiwan', *International Herald Tribune* (*IHT*), 10–11 June 1995, p. 6.

[28] Ralph Clough, *Reaching Across the Taiwan Strait: People-to-People Diplomacy* (Boulder, CO: Westview Press, 1993), p. 187.

[29] See Mark J. Valencia, *China and the South China Sea Disputes*, Adelphi Paper 298 (Oxford: OUP for the IISS, 1995).

[30] Cited in Patrick Walters, 'China Keeps Spratlys Off Forum Agenda', *The Australian*, 31 July 1995, p. 7.

[31] 'Places, Not Bases: Pacific Commander Outlines New US Defence Role', *Far Eastern Economic Review*, vol. 156, no. 16, 22 April 1993, p. 22.

[32] See the interview with Thai Second Army Region commander Lieutenant-General Surayut Chulanon, in *Athit* (Bangkok), 18–24 November 1994, in *FBIS*-EAS, 30 December 1994, pp. 81–84. Surayat notes that US war matériel is already stored at Thai armouries, but it cannot be removed without Thai government permission. The US request to pre-position additional supplies apparently involved compensating for the loss of stockpile sites at various US bases in the Philippines. See also William Branigin, 'Philippines Raise A Storm Over US Port-of-Call Accord', *IHT*, 23 November 1994, p.

6; and Elaine Sciolino, 'With Thai Rebuff, US Defers Plan for Navy Depot in Asia', *New York Times*, 12 November 1994, p. 6.

[33] Michael Leifer, 'Chinese Economic Reform and Security Policy: The South China Sea Connection', *Survival*, vol. 37, no. 2, Summer 1995, p. 57.

[34] 'Japan May Be Sucked Into S. China Sea Dispute', *Japan Times Weekly*, 1–7 May 1995, p. 3; Denny Roy, 'Hegemon on the Horizon?', *International Security*, vol. 19, no. 1, Summer 1994, pp. 163–64; and Philip Bowring, 'In South China Sea, Worrying Noises From Beijing', *IHT*, 21 July 1992, p. 4.

[35] See Ling Yu, 'The Situation On Nansha (Spratly) Islands is Tense, Sino-Philippine War May Break Out At Any Moment', in *FBIS*-CHI, 95-088, 8 May 1995, p. 9; and Valencia, *South China Sea Disputes*, pp. 44–48.

[36] Cao Baojian and Ding Feng, 'Years of Efforts by a South Sea Fleet Naval Base Results in Integrating the Procurement, Supply and Transportation of Materials to Nansha into a System', *Jiefangjun Bao* (Liberation Army Journal), in *FBIS*-CHI, 95-056, 18 March 1995, p. 33.

[37] Quoted by Amitav Acharya, *A New Regional Order in South-east Asia: ASEAN in the Post-Cold War Era*, Adelphi Paper 279 (London: Brassey's for the IISS, 1994), p. 36.

[38] See Patrick E. Tyler, 'China's Assurance on Spratlys', *IHT*, 22 May 1995, p. 9; and Valencia, *South China Sea Disputes*, pp. 23–24.

[39] This policy course has been recommended by China's Oceanic Law Society for some time. See Sheng Lijun, *China's Policy Toward the Spratly Islands in the 1990s*, Working Paper no. 287 (Canberra: Strategic and Defence Studies Centre, Australian National University, 1995), pp. 20–21.

[40] See Bill Tarrant, 'China Seen Defusing Tensions in South China Sea', *Reuters World Service*, 2 August 1995.

[41] See Winston Lord, press briefing in USIS, *Wireless File,* 17 May 1995; and Valencia, *South China Sea Disputes*, p. 25.

[42] This interpretation is discussed by Barry Wain, 'Lawyers Say Vietnam Has a Strong Case', *Asian Wall Street Journal,* 20 July 1994, p. 5. The US position would nonetheless be much stronger if it had already ratified UNCLOS. The treaty is currently awaiting ratification, but as Ann Hollick has recently observed, 'delays to Senate approval are more likely to be a function of domestic political considerations than of the merits of the treaty'. See 'Ocean Law: Senate Approval of the UN Convention', *INSS Strategic Forum*, no. 41, August 1995, p. 2.

[43] Gary Hufbauer and Jeffrey J. Schott, 'Toward Free Trade and Investment in the Asia-Pacific', *The Washington Quarterly*, vol. 18, no. 3, Summer 1995, p. 39.

[44] See Washington Post/ABC News Poll in Don Oberdorfer, 'US–Japanese Ties: A Deepening Anger', *IHT*, 2 March 1992, p. 3. According to a more recent survey, the proportion of US respondents who believe that US–Japan relations are either 'excellent' or 'pretty good' has declined from about 60% in 1991 to about 40% in 1994. See 'the Fading of Japanophobia', *The Economist*, 6 August 1994, pp. 21–22.

[45] See results of Gallup poll in, 'Poll: Many in US Indifferent Toward Japan', *Nikkei Weekly*, 8 May 1995, p. 2.

[46] See Lord's statement in, 'US Warns of Trade Link to Security', *The Australian*, 29 May 1995, p. 7.

[47] 'Congressional Report Pessimistic on Japan Relations', *Japan Times*, 14 April 1995, p. 3.

[48] *Tokyo Sankei Shimbun*, 29 January 1995, pp. 1 and 5, in *FBIS-CHI*, 95-019, 30 January 1995, pp. 1–2.

[49] See Gerald Segal, 'Tying China Into the International System', *Survival*, vol. 37, no. 2, Summer 1995, p. 65.

[50] See excerpts of the Group's report to the APEC summit in Seattle, Washington, in November 1993, in 'Now Lets Build an Asia-Pacific Economic Community', *IHT*, 4 November 1993, p. 4.

[51] 'Remarks to the Seattle-APEC Host Committee, November 19, 1993', *Weekly Compilation of Presidential Documents*, vol. 29, no. 46, 22 November 1993, p. 2400.

Chapter IV

[1] USIS, *Wireless File*, EPF200, 3 May 1994.

[2] Ministry of National Defense, Republic of Korea, *Defense White Paper 1992–1993* (English version) (Seoul: Korean Institute of Defense Analysis for the Ministry of National Defense, 1993), p. 119.

[3] 'Attack Across the DMZ', p. 24.

[4] Zhang Li, 'Fighting Back on Provocation – On the Sino-US Naval Confrontation in the Huang Hai', *Beijing Qingnian Bao*, 6 January 1995, in *FBIS*-CHI, 11 January 1995, pp. 6–7. See also, Him Mann and Art Pine, 'Faceoff Between US Ship, Chinese Sub is Revealed', *Los Angeles Times*, 14 December 1994, pp. 1 and 13–14.

[5] The concept of trust-building measures (TBMs), as opposed to confidence-building measures (CBMs), conveys a less formal approach to conflict resolution, built upon personal political contacts and relationships.

[6] These categories are covered extensively by Young-Koo Cha and Kang Choi, 'Land-Based Confidence-Building Measures in Northeast Asia: A South Korean Perspective', *The Korean Journal of Defense Analysis*, vol. 6, no. 2, Winter 1994, pp. 237–60.

[7] See Michael J. Baier, 'From Forward Defense to Forward Presence: Military Factors Influencing the ROK and US Combined Forces in the Approaching Unification Era', *Korean Journal of Defense Analysis*, vol. 6, no. 2, Winter 1994, pp. 261–84; and Cha Young-Koo, 'The Future of ROK–US Military Relations', in William J. Taylor, Jr, and Michael J. Mazarr, 'The Future of ROK–US Security Ties', in Taylor, Cha Young-Koo and John Q. Blodgett, *The Korean Peninsula: Prospects for Arms Reduction Under Global Detente* (Boulder, CO: Westview, 1990), especially pp. 107–17.

[8] 'The Jane's Interview (with Lee Yang-Ho)', *Jane's Defence Weekly*, 1 April 1995, p. 32.

[9] For example, the Clinton administration agreed in September 1994 to permit various US government officials to meet Taiwanese representatives to discuss commercial and technological issues on a 'case-by-case' basis, but not at the White House, the Pentagon or the State Department. Dick Kirchten provides a concise summary of the findings of the Clinton administration's review of US policy towards Taiwan, in 'The Other China', *The National Journal*, 8 October 1994,

pp. 2332–34.

[10] See Macke's statement in USIS, *Wireless File*, 16 February 1995, pp. 19–20. The fact that Macke resigned in November 1995 as a result of unwise statements he made with regard to the Okinawa incident does not detract from the value of his previous recommendations.

[11] See Sam Bateman, 'Build a Westpac Naval Alliance', US Naval Institute, *Proceedings*, January 1993, p. 79.

[12] For data on the projected US naval force productions, see *The Military Balance 1994–1995* (London: Brassey's for the IISS, 1994), p. 13.

[13] Quoted by Nigel Holloway in 'Jolt From the Blue', *Far Eastern Economic Review*, vol. 158, no. 31, 3 August 1995, p. 22.

[14] Michael Richardson, 'Southeast Asia Maritime Allies Gingerly Keep up Their Guard', *IHT*, 23 September 1994, p. 6.

[15] These and other proposals can be found in '"Text" of [ARF] Chairman's Statement', in *Kyodo News Agency*, in *FBIS*-EAS, 26 July 1994, p. 9; and in Desmond Ball, Richard Grant and Jusuf Wanandi, *Security Cooperation in the Asia Pacific Region* (Honolulu and Washington DC: Pacific Forum and Center for Strategic and International Studies, 1993), p. 32.

[16] ASEAN–ISIS, 'Confidence-Building Measures in South-east Asia', Memorandum no. 5, December 1993, pp. 5–6.

[17] Nye, 'The Case for Deep Engagement', p. 90.

[18] The term was coined by Segal, in 'Tying China into the International System', pp. 71–72.